THIS BOOK IS DEDICATED TO YOU:

the mums, dads, grandparents and carers. The lunchbox struggle is real and I hope this book lessens your load and makes life easier for you and your little people.

LUNCHBOX BOSS

Make mornings easier with 50+ new ideas & recipes!

George Georgievski

CONTENTS

INTRODUCTION

What am I going to put in the lunchbox today? How can I encourage my child to try new foods? Is it possible to create healthy lunchboxes that my kids will actually eat? How can I make school mornings less stressful for my family?

These are just some of the questions I've been asked over the years. Packing a balanced lunch that actually gets eaten is a massive challenge for parents, grandparents and carers — the hard slog of coming up with new ideas, trying to entice fussy eaters and catering for different dietary requirements in the family, whether it's vegan, gluten free or dairy free.

When I first started making lunchboxes for my daughters, Anela and Kiki, 7 years ago, I also felt daunted and had no idea where to start. I remember looking online for ideas, but I didn't love what I found, so I decided to create my own way of packing healthy, nutritionally balanced lunches with things I knew my girls would eat. One day, the girls brought home a note from their teacher complimenting their lunches and suggesting I post their lunchboxes on social media — and that's where @schoollunchboxdad all began.

While I've been on this amazing lunchbox journey, I've been listening, making notes and experimenting in the kitchen to find practical solutions, ideas, recipes and hacks for busy families. This book is a collection of all that I have learnt and I just know it's going to help you become the BOSS of lunchboxes in your own house.

There are more than 50 simple and delicious recipes for wraps, rolls, fritters, pastries, salads, muffins and slices — the majority of which can be whipped up in less than 30 minutes because I know how hectic mornings can be. I've also included a whole chapter on hot lunches that can be sent to school in a thermos. This can be an absolute game changer for many families (hello leftovers!).

Many more children have allergies and intolerances these days, which can be an additional challenge for families. I wanted to make things easier for parents and carers who are catering to different needs, as well as following their school's guidelines, so each recipe has notes on how to make them gluten free, dairy free, egg free, nut free and vegan. I've also included tips to entice fussy eaters as well as simple ways to increase the veg content.

I really hope this book helps you and your family to save time and reduce stress in the morning, and maybe even inspire your own lunchbox creations. Most importantly, I hope it encourages your little peeps to eat better and feel healthier and stronger — as parents and carers, that's all we could ever wish for.

On a personal level this book has given me a lot of satisfaction; downloading all the ideas and thoughts that I have collected over the years onto paper has been so rewarding. I have dedicated a lot of time and a big part of my life to my 'side hustle': a lot of travel across Australia and other parts of the world; my social media accounts; and TV and media opportunities. I love being the School Lunchbox Dad. I love it when people come up to me and ask for advice – helping people is rewarding and it fills my soul.

My girls are my life and my journey started because of them. Kiki, my youngest, is starting to spend more time in the kitchen and she has even started making her own lunches, saying: 'If Dad can do it, so can I'. Each lunchbox I make is an expression of my love for my daughters and I treat every one as though it's my last. I don't know what tomorrow will bring so I ensure I love like it's my last day. These lunchboxes are my art, they're my expression of love for my daughters through nourishing food.

I really hope this book gives you the confidence, ideas and skills to overhaul lunches in your own house, arming you with practical solutions and ideas for new ways to fill your children's lunchboxes with healthy and crazy delicious food. I know you can do it, so let's get started!

LUNCHBOX
101

HOW TO BUILD A LUNCHBOX

Start with 3 fresh veggies

- Asparagus
- Baby corn
- Beetroot
- Capsicums
- Carrots
- Celery
- Cucumbers
- Green beans
- Lettuce
- Snow or sugar snap peas
- Tomatoes

Add 2 colourful fruits

- Apples
- Apricots
- Bananas
- Berries
- Grapes
- Kiwi fruit
- Mangos
- Oranges
- Pears
- Plums
- Stone fruits
- Watermelon

Next, some nourishing wholegrains

- Baked pastries (see Life-Saving Lunchbox Bakes chapter for ideas)
- Corn tortillas or quesadillas (see page 102)
- Fritters and falafels (see pages 50, 66 and 70)
- Quinoa salads
- Savoury muffins (see page 141)
- Wholegrain wraps
- Wholegrain pastas
- Wholemeal sandwiches

Then, a little protein and/or dairy

- Edamame beans
- Eggs (hardboiled or in frittatas, see pages 136 and 146)
- Hummus or other dips
- Natural yoghurt
- Pumpkin or sunflower seeds

- Roast chicken (see page 37)
- Roasted fava beans or chickpeas
- Tasty cheese
- Tofu (great in rice paper rolls, see page 65)
- Tuna in springwater

Finish with a healthy treat

- Bliss balls (see pages 160, 167, 170 and 177)
- Crackers
- Fruit muffins (see page 156)

- Low-salt popcorn or pretzels
- Muesli bars (see pages 153 and 172)

And don't forget the reusable water bottle!

TOP TIPS TO ENSURE LUNCH GETS EATEN

Create a rainbow

Kids eat with their eyes, so use vibrant fruits and veggies to entice them and to get the visual senses going. Vary the colours and see how much of a rainbow you can create in their lunchbox.

Make it bite sized

Here's a little fact I discovered with my girls. If they can pop food in their mouth without having to bite it into pieces, they're more likely to eat it. Some bite-sized fruits and veggies that need no cutting at all:

- Berries (blueberries, raspberries)
- Cherry tomatoes
- Grapes
- Kiwi berries
- Mini capsicums
- Mini carrots
- Qukes (baby cucumbers)

Keep it fresh

No one wants to eat soggy or limp veggies, so keeping them fresh by storing them in airtight containers in the fridge is a sure-fire way to make them more appealing.

Have fun with shapes

Cutting food into shapes is a great way to encourage kids to try it, especially for younger ones. I have round, star and heart-shaped cutters to make shapes with fruit and even cheese. A melon baller is a great tool for creating bite-sized balls of fruit!

Keep things separate

There's nothing worse than a sandwich that has gone soggy from sitting next to slices of pear! Putting food items in different compartments in a bento-style lunchbox really helps to make everything more appealing come lunchtime.

Tap into your creativity when making lunchboxes! An interesting and varied lunch is fun for kids, too, and means they're more likely to eat it.

TIME-SAVING HACKS

Wash and prepare your produce

After you've done your fruit and veggie shop for the week, wash and store them ready to go in airtight containers. It keeps them fresher and means you will always have healthy lunchbox items on hand.

Batch cook on the weekend

This is another great way to save time. For example, make my muesli bars (see page 172) in a double batch and freeze them for up to 1 month.

Put your air fryer to work

This is such a time saver in the mornings when you need to cook or reheat things fast. Nearly all of the baked recipes in this book can be prepared in an air fryer.

Use a protein shaker

I find this saves me time and mess when making batters for healthy muffins for the lunchbox (see pages 141 and 156).

Roast a whole chook

This is a great way to prepare for the week ahead, as chicken can be used in so many ways in the lunchbox (see pages 100 and 114 for ideas to get you started). I've also included my go-to roast chicken recipe for you (see page 37).

Pre-cook your rice

Grab the rice cooker and steam up some rice to use the next day. Once you cook a batch of rice, cool it as quickly as possible (ideally within 1 hour – this is easily done by spreading the rice over large shallow trays until it cools). Keep the rice in the fridge for no more than 1 day until reheating. Or, even better, freeze it in ready-to-use portions for up to 1 month. When you reheat rice, always check that it's steaming hot all the way through. And do not reheat rice more than once.

MONEY-SAVING TIPS

Create a meal plan

Having a meal plan and shopping list before heading to the shops will mean less wasted produce at the end of the week. It also stops you from purchasing unnecessary items that aren't on the list! Walking down the aisles at the shops can trigger cravings for less-than-healthy foods, so you may like to try shopping online so that you buy just what's needed for your meal plan.

Hunt for bargains

Shopping online can also be cheaper, as online discounts and specials are huge. Look for meat near its expiry date for cheap deals, then freeze it to use at a later date.

Visit your green grocer

For fresh produce, go to your local green grocer. I save on average $20–25 a week by going direct to my green grocer. The produce is usually fresher, too. They will often have a section for fruit and veg that have a few spots and scuffs, called 'imperfect produce'. It's a great way to pick up heavily discounted items that tastes just as good!

Go seasonal when you can

Seasonality can make a huge difference to price – when a fruit or veg is in season, it will be cheaper and more delicious, so choose produce when the price is lower and it's abundant.

Store produce in airtight containers

This saves on wastage and, therefore, money. When I get back from the green grocer I wash the fruit and veg and store them in airtight containers in the fridge. For bigger items, such as bunches of herbs, celery or kale, wash them well, then wrap them up in damp tea towels and place in the crisper. This will extend their life by double!

Refrigerate your bread

In some climates, especially northern Australia, bread doesn't last too long in the pantry because of the heat and humidity. If you live in one of these areas, you might want to consider storing your bread in the fridge, to prevent it from going mouldy, and saving on waste and money.

Make the most of leftovers

Sometimes I will intentionally overcook for dinner, especially when I'm making spaghetti bolognese or stir-fry, knowing that my girls love them in thermoses for lunch the next day. Doing this towards the end of the week when the fridge and pantry are running low makes lunches easier and more cost effective.

Buy a good-quality lunchbox

If you invest in one of these, there'll be no need for plastic wrappers, ziplock bags and paper bags. When you use a good-quality lunchbox, you reduce the amount of packaging that goes into landfill and also save money – a win-win!

Use a refillable water bottle

This saves money and avoids more plastic going into landfill.

Make sure you don't throw out those bread crusts! See page 162 for an ingenious way to turn uneaten crusts into a delicious treat for the lunchbox.

GET THE KIDS INVOLVED

Take them shopping

Taking my girls to the supermarket and green grocer was a game changer.
I asked them to choose their apples and any other fruit for their lunchbox. Giving
them the responsibility of picking their produce gives them a sense of ownership.
It also gives you the power of saying: 'you picked it, you eat it!'.

Cook together

Choose an easy recipe from this book and get your little peeps to help you make
it. Let them enjoy the process and enjoy what they make. You never know, they
might fall in love with cooking. Start them young and get them their own apron to
make it feel special!

Grow your own

Respecting food is a big deal in my family. Teaching my girls about the time and
effort needed to grow the fruit and veggies that end up in their lunchbox has
made them appreciate this fresh produce – and more likely to eat it! All you need
is a small pot, some soil and a few seeds.

EQUIPMENT ESSENTIALS

Bento-style lunchbox

A good lunchbox is key. There are loads of great options available these days. I use a Yumbox, which is leakproof and has separate compartments that stop cross contamination of food. This is essential for kids to enjoy their lunch.

A helpful tip I have learnt along the lunchbox journey is to use the lunchbox at home first for a month or so prior to school commencing. It is a great way to get your kids used to eating from it and to learn how to open and close it. I sometimes even use the Yumbox as a dinner tray for my girls!

Cooler bag and ice pack

I always pop the lunchbox in a cooler bag with an ice block. It keeps the lunch cool and fresh well into the school day.

Water bottle

I recommend a good-quality water bottle that's not too heavy. I drop in a few ice cubes on warmer days and every other day I also squeeze in a few drops of lemon juice. Choose a drink bottle that has the lid attached to it — missing lids freak me out.

The daily intake as recommended by Health Direct Australia is as follows:

4 to 8 year olds: 5 cups
9 to 13 year olds: 5–6 cups
14 to 18 year olds: 6–8 cups

Thermos

A kid-friendly thermos is essential for taking warm foods to school. I suggest getting one with a large opening so that your kids can get their hand in. It's so easy to fill the thermos with healthy leftovers from the night before — or try some of my gold-class lunches that are designed to be sent to school in a thermos (see pages 116, 120, 124 and 132 for ideas).

The trick to making sure the food stays warm is to fill the thermos with boiling water first and close the lid so the internal lining of the stainless-steel heats up. Let it sit for 10 minutes before draining then adding the hot food and closing the lid tightly.

MANAGING DIETARY REQUIREMENTS

It's common these days to have one or more dietary requirements among children in a family, and many schools have a nut-free policy for lunches as this is one of the more common allergies among children. I wanted the recipes in this book to be used by as wide a range of people as possible, so they are almost entirely nut free and there are loads of gluten-free, dairy-free, vegetarian and vegan options.

I've used the following key to show the dietary information for each recipe. You can also find suggestions for replacing ingredients in the notes at the bottom of each recipe, or use my replacement suggestions below to sub ingredients in and out to make the recipes work for your own family.

GF ➞ GLUTEN FREE

NF ➞ NUT FREE

DF ➞ DAIRY FREE

EF ➞ EGG FREE

V ➞ VEGETARIAN

VG ➞ VEGAN

EGGS

When egg is used as a binder in a baking recipe, you can replace 1 egg with any of the following:

- 1 tablespoon of flaxseeds or chia seeds mixed with 3 tablespoons of water (leave it for 15 minutes to thicken)
- 4 tablespoons of mashed banana (for sweet recipes)
- 1 tablespoon of chickpea flour mixed with 3 tablespoons of water
- 1 tablespoon of cornflour mixed with 3 tablespoons of water
- 3 tablespoons of chickpea water from the can (aquafaba). If your chickpea liquid is too thin, just reduce it in a saucepan until it thickens to the same consistency as egg whites.

MILK

Replace cow's milk with any of the following:

- Almond milk (if your school allows nuts)
- Cashew milk (if your school allows nuts)
- Coconut milk
- Oat milk
- Rice milk
- Soy milk

CHEESE

Replace cheese with any of the following:

- Cashew cheese (if your school allows nuts)
- Hummus or avocado (if on a sandwich or cracker)
- Nutritional yeast flakes
- Pesto
- Tahini
- Vegan cheese (many varieties available; check if they contain nuts)

MEAT

Replace meat with any of the following:

- Cauliflower
- Chickpeas
- Eggplant
- Kidney beans
- Lentils
- Mushrooms
- Smoked/marinated tofu or tempeh
- Young jackfruit (available in cans from the supermarket)

SANDWICHES, WRAPS AND ROLLS

KIKI'S TUNA MAYO MIX

Do your kids get bored of having the same sandwich fillings day in day out? Kiki, my youngest, asked me to get creative with tuna. This fun filling can be added to any wrap, sandwich or even lettuce cups, as I have done here. It is super healthy and so easy to whip up that these days Kiki makes it for herself.

2 x 95 g cans of tuna (in springwater)

120 g (½ cup) mayonnaise

¼ red onion, finely diced

¼ cup finely chopped flat-leaf parsley leaves

8 iceberg lettuce leaves, washed and dried

Makes 8

GF NF DF

Put the tuna (it's okay if some of the springwater goes in), mayo, red onion and parsley in a mixing bowl and give it a really good stir with a fork — you want the tuna to be completely covered in the mayo.

Divide the filling among the lettuce leaf cups and pop them in the lunchbox. It's as simple as that.

Pop the lunchbox into a cooler bag with an ice block.

TIP

This tuna mix can be added to a roll, sandwich or wrap. You could even use it in a sushi roll.

Gluten free

Make sure the mayo is gluten free if your kids have intolerances.

Egg free

Egg-free mayo is readily available at supermarkets and works well here.

Fussy eaters

Swap out the red onion for spring onion or chives for a milder taste, or omit it entirely. Swap the tuna for shredded roast chicken if your kids don't love tuna.

Tuna mayo in lettuce cups (see page 30) is such a fresh and healthy lunch. If your child isn't into lettuce, you can use the tuna mayo mix in a sandwich or wrap instead.

Fill these little bread dumplings with whatever your child loves — ham and cheese is usually a winner.

AVOCADO CONES

**This is as close to savoury ice cream as you'll ever get.
And what kid doesn't like ice cream? The best thing about this recipe
is that you can change up the flavours anytime you like,
just like ice cream. Let's rock.**

4 mini flatbreads or flour tortillas

4 slices of cheddar

4 slices of ham

4 wooden skewers

2 avocados

50 g (¼ cup) chopped cherry tomatoes, plus 4 whole

lemon juice (optional)

Makes 4

NF EF

You can cook the flatbreads in an air fryer or the oven. If cooking in the oven, preheat to 180°C fan-forced. Line a baking tray with baking paper.

Place the flatbreads on the baking tray and top each one with a slice of cheese and a slice of ham. Now, I want you think about an ice cream cone – that's what we are about to create. Roll the flatbread up with the ingredients inside so it has a pointy end (remember: think cone) and an open end. Grab a skewer and pierce it right through so the shape holds. Pop the cones into the oven to cook for 6 minutes. If using an air fryer, cook at 180°C for 3 minutes.

In the meantime, scoop the avocado flesh into a ziplock bag, expelling as much air as possible, and seal the seam. Bash the avo around until it is mashed and there are no big bits. We are going to use the ziplock bag as a piping bag, so stand by.

Once the cones are out of the oven, remove the skewers. Put the four whole cherry tomatoes aside, then distribute the chopped cherry tomato among the cones.

Snip the bottom corner off the ziplock bag with scissors – you're about to become a piping master. Start filling the cones with the avo – when you get to the top you can add a decorative swirl or two. Now add the pièce de résistance: the cherry (tomato) on top.

Place two cones head-to-tail side by side in each lunchbox – they will sit nice and snug like this and won't spill. Add a squeeze of lemon juice to the avo to keep it greener for longer, if you like.

Gluten free
Gluten-free flatbreads also work a treat here – these days there are so many to choose from.

Dairy free
Sub in plant-based cheddar to make a dairy-free wrap.

Vego/vegan
You can replace the ham with facon (fake bacon) or marinated tofu for a vego option. And go one step further and sub in plant-based cheese for vegan.

Fussy eaters
The concept of having lunch in a cone is what little humans love – feel free to fill them with your fussy eater's fave ingredients. A simple ham, cheese and lettuce trio could also be used.

THE BEST ROAST CHICKEN FOR SANDWICHES & WRAPS

**Here is my version of roast chook for next-day school lunches —
be it sandwich fillings, wraps or salads.**

1 x 1.7 kg whole chicken

3 tablespoons extra-virgin olive oil

1 tablespoon garlic powder

1 teaspoon sea salt

1 tablespoon smoked paprika

Serves 6–8

GF NF DF EF

Preheat the oven to 185°C fan-forced and get out a large baking tray.

Grab your chook and a pair of kitchen scissors. The quickest way to cook a chicken is by using the butterfly technique. Place the chook breast-side down and cut from the tail to the neck either side of the spine. Remove the spine, then place the chicken on the baking tray breast-side up. Push down on the breasts to flatten the chook out.

Place the olive oil and spices in a cup or small bowl and give them a good mix with a small whisk or fork. Brush the mixture all over the chicken, being sure to get a nice even coverage. Pop it in the oven and cook for 45 minutes.

When the chook is ready, take it out and let it rest for about 20 minutes — not because you should rest your cooked poultry, but because you need to skin it and it will be too hot to handle. After you've removed the skin, shred the chicken, placing the dark meat strips to one side of an airtight container and the white meat strips on the other — when I make sandwiches I use a combination of both, but some children prefer just the white meat. Discard the bones and skin.

When using the shredded chicken, be sure to put the lunchbox inside a cooler bag with an ice block to keep the temp of the chicken below 4°C.

TIP

The chicken will keep in the fridge for up to 4 days. Check out my Cuban Salada melts (see page 100) and mini roast chicken tacos (see page 114) for some roast chook inspiration.

QUICK & EASY VEGEMITE SCROLLS

If you've never taken a Vegemite scroll to school you're missing out on a great Australian culinary experience. There are so many variations of the Vegemite scroll, but I usually use wholemeal bread for this fun creation (you can use any bread that rocks your little peeps). A prerequisite for this recipe is to ensure that the Vegemite jar has a thousand crumbs inside it.

8 slices of bread

50 g unsalted butter, softened

2–3 tablespoons Vegemite, or to taste

4 wooden skewers

Makes 4

NF EF V

TIPS

If you like, you can wrap the scrolls in foil so that they're still warm for lunchtime.

You can prepare these the night before, leaving them in an airtight container overnight. All you need to do is toast them in the morning and you're done.

First, cut the crusts off the bread, but don't throw them out (you can use them to make strawberry jam crust roll-ups on page 162). Pop two bread slices on a chopping board side by side but overlapping by 1 cm. Use a rolling pin to roll them together. You should now have a squashed bread rectangle. Repeat with the remaining bread slices to create four rectangles.

Smear butter, then Vegemite, on the bread rectangles, making sure it's evenly distributed among them.

Time to make the scrolls. Using both hands, lift the long side of a bread rectangle and firmly roll it up to look like a snake. Now you'll need to create the scroll. Starting at one end, coil the snake inwards to look like a large snail. Use a skewer to hold the scroll together while you make the remaining scrolls.

You can pack these scrolls in a lunchbox the way they are, no problem. But! If you want to take them to the next level, pop them in the toaster so the skewers are sticking up out of the toaster (please don't use metal skewers!) and toast them. Once toasted, you can add a little extra butter on top and perhaps a dash of Vegemite for garnish. Very fancy indeed.

Remove the skewers before popping into the lunchbox — the scrolls will hold their shape perfectly.

Gluten free

Gluten-free bread works a treat in this recipe.

Dairy free/vegan

Dairy-free butter is an amazing sub for real butter. Nuttelex with coconut oil is a great palm oil–free option.

Fussy eaters

The shape is the key for this recipe — kids love fun shapes. You can use whatever fillings your little peeps prefer. Hazelnut-flavoured spread comes to mind ...

CHEESY BAKED COBB LOAVES

Cobb loaves are the bomb. The cheese, the bread, the fun ... it's delicious and exciting all at once. The trick to turning the cobb loaf buzz into a lunchbox hit is to use dinner rolls. There are so many variations you can make using this recipe – bolognese, pizza, mac 'n' cheese, not to mention sweet versions. Today I am making the easiest mini Hawaiian pizza loaves ever.

4 dinner rolls

1 tablespoon salt-free tomato paste

75 g (½ cup) grated mozzarella

60 g (½ cup) grated cheddar

4 slices of smoked bacon, chopped

65 g (⅓ cup) pineapple pieces (fresh or canned)

Makes 4

NF EF

You can cook these in an air fryer or the oven. If cooking in the oven, preheat to 180°C fan-forced. Line a baking tray with baking paper.

Cut the tops off the rolls with a bread knife and put the tops, crumb-side up, on the baking tray. Pull some (but not all) of the bread out of the rolls with your fingers. (You can pop this bread in a ziplock bag and freeze it to make croutons or breadcrumbs with later.) Now, use your fingers to press down the inside of each roll to create a secure little bread chamber.

Drop 1 teaspoon of the tomato paste into each roll and spread it all around with the back of a spoon. Mix the cheeses and bacon together in a small bowl, then divide them evenly between the rolls. Add a tablespoon of the pineapple pieces and give it all a nice mix so the pineapple isn't just sitting up top.

Place the rolls on the baking tray with the bread tops and bake for 15 minutes, or until the cheese is melted and the buns are slightly charred. If using an air fryer, cook at 180°C for 8–9 minutes.

Place the lids on the rolls. You can serve these at room temp or warm. If serving warm, wrap the hot rolls in foil and pop them straight into the lunchbox. Enjoy.

Gluten free
Sub in mini gluten-free rolls instead of the dinner rolls.

Dairy free
Use your favourite mix of plant-based cheeses in place of the cheddar and mozzarella.

Vego/vegan
Vegetarians can leave the bacon out or sub it with an alternative. To make these vegan, you'll also need to sub in plant-based cheese.

Extra veg
You can hide finely chopped veggies, such as capsicum, mushroom or onion, in the base of the mini cobb loaves. Fresh herbs work well, too – add basil leaves for a pizza vibe.

Fussy eaters
I have made bolognese and mac 'n' cheese versions of these and they were a huge hit. The great thing about this recipe is that fussy eaters can't see what's in the bottom of the mini cobb loaves. Wink wink.

These date and almond bliss balls (see page 167) are a brilliant addition as they are high in protein. If your child can't take nuts to school, see pages 153 and 177 for nut-free options.

Crispy, crunchy and totally moreish — you can't beat a nacho sandwich (see page 47).

BEST-EVER CHICKEN MAYO MIX

While I'd like to take complete credit for this recipe, I'll let you in on a little secret: when I was 15 I worked at Red Rooster. It was there that I really began to love cooking and I learnt all about the versatility of chicken. This mix can be used as a filling for a heap of lunchbox additions, such as wraps, sandwiches and rolls.

1 whole hot supermarket roast chicken

1 long celery stalk, finely chopped

¼ cup finely chopped flat-leaf parsley leaves

250 g (1 cup) mayonnaise

1 teaspoon smoked paprika

juice of ½ lemon

Serves 6–8

NF DF

First things first: you'll need to get your hands dirty and remove the skin from the supermarket chook – it's best done when lukewarm. Remove the stuffing from the carcass and set it aside on a chopping board with the chicken.

Pop the celery and parsley into a large mixing bowl. Shred the chicken into small strips with your hands so that the pieces will fit nicely into a sandwich or wrap (I like to cut them into different sizes) and add them to the bowl.

Now, the crazy part: divide the reserved stuffing in half (you only need half). It should be crumbly, if not, just cut it up nice and small before dropping it in the mixing bowl. Add the mayo, smoked paprika and lemon. Give it a good old mix until all the ingredients are combined. Naturally, you will need to taste test, so adjust the seasoning as you desire.

When using the chicken mayo mix, make sure you pack it in an airtight container inside a cooler bag with an ice block to keep the temp of the chicken below 4°C.

TIP

This chicken mayo mix will keep in an airtight container in the fridge for up to 5 days.

Gluten free

Instead of the chook stuffing, you could use ½ cup of gluten-free stuffing with a pinch of salt and a teaspoon of olive oil. Lay it out on a baking tray and bake it in a preheated 240°C oven for 10 minutes.

Egg free

Opt for egg-free mayonnaise.

Vegan

Sub in vegan mayo and plant-based chicken strips. Always check plant-based chicken alternatives to ensure they're not filled with chemicals and numbers.

Extra veg

Add ½ cup of finely chopped cucumber to the mix.

Fussy eaters

Serve the chicken mayo mix in cute bite-sized sandwiches.

NACHO SANDWICHES

This would have to be my favourite sandwich creation ever and I've been lucky enough for this recipe to be featured a few times in food blogs around the world.

1 cup corn chips

1 egg

4 thick slices of bread

3 tablespoons natural yoghurt

1 tomato, sliced

2 slices of cheddar

GUACAMOLE

1 avocado, mashed

¼ red onion, finely diced

½ cup chopped coriander leaves (optional)

1 teaspoon extra-virgin olive oil

juice of 1 lime wedge

pinch of sea salt

Makes 2

NF V

You can cook these in an air fryer or the oven. If cooking in the oven, preheat to 180°C fan-forced. Line a baking tray with baking paper.

Place the corn chips in a ziplock bag, expelling as much air as possible, and seal the seam. Smash the corn chips with a rolling pin until they're about 5 mm in size, then pour them onto a plate.

Crack the egg into a wide shallow bowl and whisk it until combined. Dip the slices of bread into the egg wash on one side and then straight into the crushed corn chips. Place the bread on the baking tray, corn-chip side up, and pop into the oven to cook for 5–7 minutes, or until the corn chips are toasted and lightly browned. If using an air fryer, cook at 180°C for 5 minutes.

While the bread is toasting, mix the guacamole ingredients in a bowl until combined.

To assemble, place a slice of the bread, corn-chip side down, on a chopping board. Spread a few tablespoons of the guacamole onto the bread, drizzle with some yoghurt, add a couple of tomato slices and then the cheese. Pop the other slice on top – corn-chip side facing outwards – and cut in half. Yummo.

TIP

This recipe can be prepared the night before. Store the corn-chip covered bread slices in an airtight container in the pantry. To keep the guac fresh, put it in an airtight container and drizzle extra-virgin olive oil on top so it coats the surface. Pop it in the fridge and assemble everything in the morning.

Gluten free

Gluten-free bread works a treat in this recipe and make sure the corn chips you use are gluten free.

Dairy free

Use plant-based yoghurt and cheese slices.

Fussy eaters

Tempt your picky eaters by ditching the coriander and red onion in the guacamole.

SAVOURY BALLS, FRITTERS AND BITES

GREEN PEA FRITTERS

More veggies and less batter is always better when making these. My daughter Kiki loves them, especially when dipped in mint yoghurt — but you can leave that out to make them even easier to prepare. Green pea fritters are a great summer lunch that can be eaten hot or cold.

310 g (2 cups) frozen peas

2 eggs

1 teaspoon sea salt

75 g (½ cup) self-raising flour

3 tablespoons extra-virgin olive oil

MINTY YOGHURT DIP

1 tablespoon chopped mint leaves

130 g (½ cup) natural yoghurt

Makes 8–10

NF V

How do we make these bad boys green? Place half the peas in a food processor with the eggs, salt and flour and blitz it all up till it's Incredible Hulk green (it should look like a green thickshake). Transfer the mixture to a bowl, add the rest of the peas and stir until all the peas are thoroughly mixed through.

Prepare a large plate lined with baking paper to place the fritters on as you make them. Scoop the mixture out with a tablespoon, then use your hands to shape individual patties — you can make them whatever size you like.

Before you start frying, line a large plate with paper towel. Heat the olive oil in a frying pan over medium heat. Fry the patties in batches for around 2 minutes on each side, or until they're golden brown. Once cooked, place the patties on the paper towel to remove any excess oil.

To make the very complicated yoghurt dip, just mix the mint leaves and yoghurt together in a small bowl. Pop the yoghurt dip in a spillproof tub for dipping.

TIPS

These can be made the night before and will keep in an airtight container in the fridge for 3–4 days.

To make these orange instead of green, just swap out the peas for carrots, but you'll need to blanch the carrots first to soften them up. Pick your fave vegetable and the sky's the limit. Zucchini fritters are great too, or you can blend and mix different types of veggies for superfood fritters.

Gluten free
You can replace the self-raising flour with gluten-free self-raising flour in this recipe.

Dairy free
To make these dairy-free, replace the yoghurt dip with sweet chilli sauce or coconut yoghurt with ½ teaspoon of salt added.

NO-FUSS BEEF PATTIES

Once a week I make killer cheeseburgers for dinner – it's a fun casual dinner where I smash some burgers together and we indulge. My daughter Anela once took the leftovers to school and they were such a hit – even with her friends – that I have modified the recipe to make them lunchbox friendly. See page 126 for how to use these patties to make beef sliders.

500 g beef mince

1 egg

50 g (½ cup) dried breadcrumbs

1 teaspoon sea salt

1 teaspoon onion powder

olive oil, for cooking

Makes 8

NF DF

Put the mince in a large mixing bowl. Now this is going to sound nuts, but I let it warm up a little (for around 1 hour) because when I mix it up my fingers freeze and it's not cool … well, it is cool, but you know what I'm saying, right?

Drop in the rest of the ingredients in any order you like. Wash your hands before mixing the ingredients with your hands.

Prepare a large plate or tray lined with baking paper to place the patties as you make them. Use wet hands to make the patties so that the mixture doesn't stick to your fingers. I make eight balls, then squash them on the grill when I start cooking. (I use a barbecue grill, however a frying pan works perfectly well, too.)

Drizzle a little olive oil into the pan or on the barbecue grill and line a large plate with paper towel. The cooking time depends on how flat you squash the patties; I like them crispy, so I squash them till they're about 1 cm thick. The cooking time for 1 cm thick patties is around 3 minutes on each side.

I usually cook these the night before and pop them in an airtight container in the fridge once they cool down. In the morning, microwave them for 2 minutes so they're super hot and then put them straight into a hot thermos (see Tips).

TIPS

Once cooked, these beef patties will keep in an airtight container in the fridge for 3–4 days.

To keep the patties nice and hot, fill a thermos with boiling water and close the lid so the internal lining of the stainless steel heats up. Let it sit for 10 minutes before replacing the hot water with the hot food.

Gluten free
Use your favourite gluten-free breadcrumbs.

Egg free
Replace the egg with 1 tablespoon of milk.

These crispy zucchini fritters (see page 70) are a great way to get a serve of veg into your kids at lunchtime!

Most kids love bite-sized foods, like these delicious vegetable rice balls (see page 56).

VEGETABLE RICE BALLS

These vegan rice balls are super cute and so tasty. You can use steamed rice from the night before, or a packet of microwave rice will also work.

185 g (1 cup) steamed rice

80 g (½ cup) grated carrot

40 g (¼ cup) finely chopped red onion

40 g (¼ cup) green peas

90 g (½ cup) rice flour

1 teaspoon salt flakes

170 ml (⅔ cup) vegetable oil

mayo and soy sauce, to serve (optional)

Makes 15

NF DF EF VG

Grab your fave mixing bowl and drop in all the ingredients except the vegetable oil. Add 3 tablespoons of water and use your hands to mix the ingredients so that you can squeeze the rice and feel if it needs a little more water or not. Mix until the ingredients are well combined and the rice has become dough-like.

Prepare a large plate or tray lined with baking paper to place the balls as you make them – this recipe makes around 15 balls. Roll the balls to the size of a table tennis ball: big enough to fit in a little human's hand and small enough to fit in the lunchbox.

Before you start frying, line a large plate with paper towel. Place a large frying pan over medium heat and add the vegetable oil. Place half the rice balls in the pan, being careful not to overcrowd them. Cook for 3–4 minutes, until nice and golden, then turn them over and cook for 3 minutes more, until cooked evenly all over. Repeat until all the rice balls are cooked. Place them on the paper towel to drain off any excess oil. You could also cook these in an air fryer at 180°C for 8–10 minutes.

Pop the rice balls straight into a preheated thermos (see Tips). If you like, serve with a side of mayo or even add some soy sauce to the mayo. Your kids are going to love these.

TIPS

To keep the rice balls nice and hot, fill a thermos with boiling water and close the lid so the internal lining of the stainless steel heats up. Let it sit for 10 minutes before replacing the hot water with the hot food.

My girls love a hint of wasabi in the mayo mix. As your kids get older their taste buds will develop – maybe try this when they're open to it!

Gluten free
Use gluten-free soy sauce.

Fussy eaters
The veggies can be varied to suit your little human. Leaving out the onion and using another veggie is totally cool.

PANKO-CRUMBED TUNA BALLS

Goodness gracious, tuna balls to the rescue. Tuna is an amazing source of protein, but the flavour isn't for everyone. It took a while to get my girls into it, which is why I'm sharing this gateway recipe with you. This recipe has a slight Asian vibe, but remember you can go with any combo you like.

1 tablespoon sesame oil

35 g (½ cup) panko breadcrumbs

2 x 95 g cans of tuna in springwater, drained

1 tablespoon finely sliced spring onion

1 egg

1 tablespoon soy sauce

1 teaspoon finely chopped lemongrass stalk, white part only

Makes 12

NF DF

You can cook these in an air fryer or the oven. If cooking in the oven, preheat to 180°C fan-forced. Grease a baking tray with the sesame oil. Sprinkle half the panko breadcrumbs on a plate.

Place the remaining panko breadcrumbs in a bowl, add all the other ingredients and mix well — I use a fork for this as it's easy to scrape the edge of the bowl. You'll have to test the mixture to make sure it holds together — the best way I know is to use your hands and feel if it sticks well enough to create some balls. If it's too dry add more egg, or if it's too wet add more breadcrumbs.

Using your hands, roll golf ball–sized tuna balls. Now roll the tuna balls in the panko breadcrumbs to cover them, then place them on the baking tray. Pop them in the oven for 30 minutes, turning once during cooking. They will be crispy and brown when ready. If using an air fryer, cook at 180°C for 20 minutes, turning once at the 10-minute mark.

Allow the tuna balls to cool slightly before you pop them into the lunchbox.

TIP

Once cooked, these tuna balls will keep in an airtight container in the fridge for 2–3 days. Or you can freeze them for up to 1 month.

Gluten free
Use gluten-free breadcrumbs.

Egg free
Replace the egg with chia or flaxseed mixed with water — see page 26 for more information.

Fussy eaters
If you want to simplify the flavour, omit or reduce the quantity of lemongrass and onion.

Crispy falafel (see page 66) and creamy hummus are a winning combination. Team them with a rainbow of veg for extra dipping.

Lunch is sorted with veggie frittata (see page 136) and a slice of no-bake vegan muesli bar (see page 172).

ITALIAN MEATBALLS

**Anyone who doesn't like Italian meatballs needs to call a 1800 helpline now.
I always make a double batch of these and freeze them for when I hear,
'Dad, can you make Italian meatballs?'.**

250 g pork mince

250 g beef mince

1 egg

50 g (½ cup) dried breadcrumbs

50 g (½ cup) grated parmesan

1 teaspoon dried oregano

2 garlic cloves, crushed

½ teaspoon sea salt

½ brown onion, finely chopped

2 tablespoons extra-virgin olive oil

½ cup basil leaves, finely chopped

ITALIAN TOMATO SAUCE

2 tablespoons extra-virgin olive oil

2 garlic cloves, crushed

2 x 400 g cans diced tomatoes

2 tablespoons salt-free tomato paste

1 teaspoon sea salt

Makes 10

NF

Let's get our sauce on first. Grab a large deep frying pan and put it on medium heat with the olive oil. When the oil has heated up, drop in the garlic and cook for 3–4 minutes while stirring, until it becomes lightly golden. Stir through the diced tomatoes and tomato paste. Add 125 ml (½ cup) of water to one of the tomato cans and swish it around to make sure the water collects any left-behind tomatoes, then pour this into your second can and do the same. Finally, pour the tomato water into the pan and give it a good stir, add the salt and stir again. Reduce the heat to low and pop a lid on it.

Now let's make our meatballs. Place all of the ingredients except the oil and basil in a mixing bowl and give them a really good mix with your hands. I find that it's better to take the mince out of the fridge an hour prior — this saves your fingers from freezing and it also makes the mince easier to break up.

Add the olive oil to a separate large frying pan over medium heat. Using wet hands, roll the mince to make whatever size meatballs will fit in your kids' lunchboxes — I usually work with 2 tablespoons of mixture per meatball. Drop them straight into the pan and brown on all sides — around 5–6 minutes. Drop them into the simmering sauce and cook for a further 15 minutes with the lid on. For the last minute of cooking, add the basil and mix through.

Allow the meatballs and sauce to cool before placing in an airtight container in the fridge. To reheat, simply zap a serving of meatballs and sauce in the microwave for 2 minutes and put them straight into a preheated thermos (see Tips).

TIPS

To keep the meatballs nice and hot, fill a thermos with boiling water and close the lid so the internal lining of the stainless steel heats up. Let it sit for 10 minutes before replacing the hot water with the hot food.

Cooked meatballs can be stored in an airtight container in the fridge for 3–4 days, or frozen for up to 1 month.

Gluten free	**Dairy free**	**Egg free**	**Vegan**
Use gluten-free breadcrumbs.	Opt for plant-based grated parmesan.	Replace the egg with 1 tablespoon of milk.	See page 73 for my no-meat balls recipe.

RICE PAPER ROLLS

Rice paper rolls are like the ultimate transparent sandwich. The phrase 'fresh is best' certainly applies to this recipe. There is something special about creating a lunch with colourful herbs and veggies our little peeps can see. This simple classic recipe is one where the veggies shine right through, literally.

100 g vermicelli noodles

4 rice paper sheets

handful of coriander and/or mint leaves (optional)

100 g shredded cooked chicken (see page 37 for a recipe)

1 small cucumber, cut into matchsticks

1 small carrot, cut into matchsticks

handful of shredded lettuce

1–2 tablespoons hoisin sauce

Makes 4

GF NF DF EF

Cook or soak the vermicelli noodles as per the packet instructions until soft but not mushy. Drain well.

Next, grab a dinner plate or large shallow bowl and fill it with cool water. Dip a rice paper sheet in the water for 20–30 seconds to soften (check the packet instructions as the length of time may vary). As soon as the rice paper softens, lay it on a moist tea towel and begin the wrapping.

Remember that the rice paper is transparent so it has to look good on the inside. Place one-quarter of the ingredients in the bottom third of the rice paper sheet closest to you, being sure to leave a nice clear border. I like to start with the herbs, then I add the noodles, chicken, veggies and a drizzle of hoisin sauce. To roll, pull the rice paper edge closest to you up over the ingredients like a cosy blanket. Now fold the sides in nice and snug. Finally, roll the filling so that it becomes fully enclosed. It should be nice and tight and the wet rice paper will make it stick together. Repeat the process to make three more rolls.

Pack into the lunchbox and make sure you use a cooler bag with an ice block to keep the temperature of the chicken below 4°C.

TIP

You can make these rice paper rolls the night before – they'll keep stored in an airtight container in the fridge for 2–3 days.

Gluten free

Make sure you choose a gluten-free hoisin sauce, as some brands use wheat as a thickener.

Vegan

Make these vegan by using sliced tofu instead of the shredded chicken.

Fussy eaters

These rice paper rolls are perfect for fussy kids as you can so easily mix and match to suit their preferences when it comes to veggies. Sliced capsicum, green beans and snow peas all work really well, and omit the herbs if they are too strong.

EASY FALAFELS

Okay, this is the one recipe I fear the most — not because of the recipe, but because I have a heap of Middle Eastern followers and I will hear about it if it's not up to standard. But remember, this is an easy version. Traditionally you use dried chickpeas and soak them overnight, but this is my dad-style 'let's get cracking' version.

400 g can chickpeas, drained

2 garlic cloves

2 tablespoons finely chopped flat-leaf parsley leaves

½ red onion, roughly chopped

1 teaspoon ground cumin

1 teaspoon ground coriander

1 teaspoon sea salt

3 tablespoons plain flour

1 teaspoon sesame seeds

125 ml (½ cup) vegetable oil

Makes 16

NF DF EF VG

What I love about this recipe is that the food processor does all the hard work. Place all the ingredients except the oil in the food processor and hit go. My food processor blitzes everything together in around 1 minute, but what you're looking for is a consistent blend of all the ingredients.

Prepare a large plate or tray lined with baking paper to place the falafels as you make them. Scoop a heaped tablespoon of the mixture onto the sheet of baking paper (I use a small ice cream scoop). This mix will make around 16 golf ball–sized balls. You can keep them round or flatten them slightly with the base of a glass.

Before you start frying, line a large plate with paper towel. Heat the oil in a frying pan over medium heat. Fry the falafels for around 2–3 minutes on each side, or until they are golden. Don't overcook them: hard shells on falafels aren't cool. Place the cooked falafels on the paper towel to drain. You could also cook these falafels in an air fryer on 180°C for 8 minutes, turning them once at the 4-minute mark.

Once cool, pop the falafels straight into the lunchbox.

TIPS

Add a few falafels to a garden salad or pop them in a flatbread wrap with some hummus.

These falafels will keep in an airtight container in the fridge for 5 days or frozen for 3 months.

Gluten free

Gluten-free flour would work fine in these falafels.

Fussy eaters

I use red onion because the flavour isn't as strong as brown onion, but just omit it entirely if needed. Cardamom and black pepper are also commonly used in falafels; however, I've omitted those in my recipe in favour of spices that work best for my girls. You could try introducing the extra spices by adding them in small quantities and see how they go.

Don't forget the hoisin sauce for dipping these fresh rice paper rolls into (see page 65).

Make a big batch of Italian meatballs (see page 62) and pop the leftovers in a bread roll for lunch the next day. This also works well with my no-meat balls (see page 73).

SUE-CHINI FRITTERS

**These zucchini fritters are named in honour of my sister, Sue.
Whip up a batch of these nutritious fritters and pop them in your kids'
lunchboxes for a super-healthy and tasty lunch.**

400 g (3 cups) grated zucchini

1 teaspoon sea salt

2 eggs

75 g (½ cup) plain flour

30 g (¼ cup) finely sliced
spring onion

3 tablespoons extra-virgin
olive oil

130 g (½ cup) natural yoghurt

Makes 10

NF V

Place the zucchini and salt in a large bowl and stir to combine. Set aside for 10–15 minutes for the salt to draw the moisture out of the zucchini and prevent soggy fritters. When ready, use your hands to squeeze the moisture out of the zucchini and discard the liquid.

Add the eggs, flour and spring onion to the bowl and stir to thoroughly combine – the mixture should be almost sticky.

Prepare a large plate or tray lined with baking paper to place the fritters as you make them. Scoop a couple of tablespoons of mixture for each fritter and use your hands to shape the patties.

Before you start frying, line a large plate with paper towel. Heat the oil in a frying pan over medium heat, then add the fritters. Cook for around 3 minutes, or until golden brown, then turn them over and cook for 3 minutes more. (You might need to cook these in two batches, depending on the size of your frying pan.) Place the cooked fritters on the paper towel to drain any excess oil.

Pop the fritters into the lunchbox. You can either dollop the yoghurt on top of the fritters or include it as a dip on the side in its own little spillproof container.

TIPS

The fritters will keep in an airtight container in the fridge for 2–3 days.

Making the mixture the night before and popping it into an airtight container in the fridge will save you loads of time in the morning.

Gluten free

Gluten-free plain flour is perfect with this recipe.

Dairy free

You can swap the natural yoghurt for a plant-based option.

Fussy eaters

Swapping out the yoghurt for mayo or sweet chilli sauce is an option to tempt picky kids.

NO-MEAT BALLS
(THANKS, WAZ!)

Meatballs are awesome, and these no-meat balls are just as awesome. I originally came up with this recipe for my best friend, Warren Freeman, who is vegan, but it turns out these no-meat balls are perfect for the lunchbox. Making these the night before is the key to a smooth morning.

3 tablespoons extra-virgin olive oil

1 brown onion, finely chopped

350 g mushrooms, cleaned and finely diced

3 garlic cloves, crushed

185 g (1 cup) steamed rice

100 g (1 cup) quick oats

1 teaspoon sea salt

2 tablespoons maple syrup

Makes 10

NF DF EF VG

Heat the oil in a frying pan over medium heat. Add the onion and cook for 3 minutes, or until translucent. Next, add the mushroom and cook for 8–9 minutes, until darkened, then drop in the garlic, rice, oats and salt and give it a really good stir. Add the maple syrup and stir it through for a minute or two before removing the pan from the heat.

Transfer the mixture to an ovenproof bowl and use a handheld blender to blitz it for around a minute. Cover the bowl with foil and pop the bowl in the fridge for 30 minutes.

Preheat the oven to 180°C fan-forced and line a baking tray with baking paper.

Once chilled, use a tablespoon to scoop out the mixture and roll it into golf ball–sized balls with your hands. Pop the balls straight onto the baking tray and cook for 5–7 minutes, then turn them over and cook for another 5–7 minutes. They will be the colour of cooked meat when ready. You can also cook these in an air fryer at 180°C for 12 minutes, turning once after 6 minutes.

You can serve these with Italian tomato sauce (see page 62). Drop the no-meat balls directly into the sauce.

In the morning, reheat the balls with the sauce in the microwave for 2 minutes. Transfer to a preheated thermos (see Tips).

TIPS

Once cooked, these no-meat balls will keep in an airtight container in the fridge for 3–4 days. Or freeze for up to 1 month.

To keep the food nice and hot, fill a thermos with boiling water and close the lid so the internal lining of the stainless steel heats up. Let it sit for 10 minutes before replacing the hot water with the hot food.

Gluten free
Use gluten-free quick oats.

SIMPLE SALADS AND SKEWERS

THREE Bs PASTA SALAD

Pasta is super versatile, easy to cook and fast. This pasta salad is all about basil, bocconcini and balsamic ... with a cherry (tomato) on top. What I love the most about this recipe is that your kids can choose their favourite pasta shapes and you really only need to assemble it. Over the years I've slightly adjusted this recipe to accommodate my girls' changing taste buds.

1 tablespoon salt

250 g dried pasta of your choice

150 g (1 cup) cherry tomatoes, halved or quartered

240 g (1 cup) bocconcini, drained and quartered

⅓ cup basil leaves

1 tablespoon extra-virgin olive oil

2 tablespoons balsamic vinegar

Serves 2–4

NF EF V

Putting the water on to boil is the hardest part of this recipe. Add the salt to the water before you start heating it, then follow the packet instructions to cook the pasta. Once the pasta is cooked, drain it really well and leave it to cool (remember that this is a cold pasta salad so there's no rush).

Place the tomato, bocconcini and basil in a mixing bowl.

As soon as the pasta has cooled down, toss it through the salad with tongs. Add the olive oil and balsamic for the final touch.

When I put this dish in a lunchbox, I like to place a basil leaf on top — that's what wins me parent awards with the kids.

TIPS

Adding cooked chicken breast pieces to this salad takes it to the next level, but always make sure it's refrigerated well when packing a school lunch.

You can use a simple Italian dressing instead of balsamic if you like — do what works best for your family.

Gluten free
Sub in your favourite gluten-free pasta.

Dairy free/vegan
Use plant-based bocconcini to make this pasta salad dairy free and vegan.

Extra veg
Add 1 cup of broccoli florets to the pasta with 3 minutes of cooking time left. Drain with the pasta and toss through the remaining ingredients.

HAWAIIAN PIZZA SKEWERS

When you combine two things that kids love – pizza and skewers – you have a winner. Just a couple of points that I have to get out of the way. I never ever use pineapple on pizza – it's just a no-go zone for me personally – but Kiki, my youngest, insisted that I use it here. (I have sought a United Nations pizza code exemption to allow pineapple in this recipe.)

3 slices of bread

2 tablespoons salt-free tomato paste

120 g (½ cup) small bocconcini, drained and halved

3 slices of deli ham off the bone

6 small wooden skewers

95 g (½ cup) pineapple pieces (fresh or canned)

Makes 6

NF EF

Preheat the oven grill to 240°C and line a baking tray with baking paper.

Using a smallish cookie cutter or an espresso cup, cut 3–4 circles out of each slice of bread. Smear the tomato paste over them and add half a bocconcini ball on top. Place the circles on the baking tray and pop them under the grill to melt the cheese a little and to toast the bread. This should take around 2–3 minutes.

Cut the ham using the same sized cookie cutter and fold the circles in half.

Time to assemble. First, thread a toasted bread circle onto a skewer, followed by a piece of folded ham and (controversially) a chunk of pineapple. Repeat the whole process again to fill up the skewer. Repeat to make six Hawaiian pizza skewers.

These are best made fresh and popped straight into the lunchbox.

TIP

Be sure to snip the points off the wooden skewers with some scissors so that the little peeps don't accidentally stab anyone with them.

Gluten free
Use gluten-free bread.

Dairy free
Use plant-based bocconcini.

Vego/vegan
To make these vego, sub in baked portobello mushrooms for the ham. Sprinkle with garlic powder, salt and a little smoked paprika for a smoky flavour. Also sub in plant-based bocconcini for vegan.

Skip sandwiches and go for this simple pasta salad (see page 76). You can choose any fun pasta shape you like.

Roast a whole chook on the weekend (see page 37 for a recipe) then use it in so many different ways in the lunchbox, from mini sandwiches to wraps and lettuce cups.

ROASTED PUMPKIN & SPINACH SALAD

This was inspired by my sister Suzy. We had dinner at her house one night and I loved this salad so much I requested the leftovers for my lunch the next day. Well, let me tell you, it tasted even better the next day. I often make this for myself and my youngest, Kiki, as she loves the roast pumpkin.

700 g butternut pumpkin

3 tablespoons honey

1 teaspoon sea salt

80 g (½ cup) pine nuts

135 g (3 cups) baby spinach leaves, washed thoroughly

1 tablespoon balsamic glaze

Serves 4–6

DF EF V

Preheat the oven to 180°C fan-forced and line a large baking tray with baking paper.

Cut the pumpkin in half vertically. Scoop the seeds from the pumpkin, then place it flat-side down and use a super-sharp knife to slice it into 1.5 cm wide wedges – you should have around 15. Peel the wedges then cut each piece in half so you turn one big wedge into two smaller wedges. Place the wedges on the baking tray and drizzle the honey over them so there is even coverage. Sprinkle the salt on top to counterbalance the sweetness. Pop the pumpkin into the oven and cook for 25 minutes or until nice and soft.

Lightly toast the pine nuts in a dry frying pan over medium heat for around 2 minutes, shaking the pan to prevent burning, until they are lightly coloured – they will continue to cook after you take them off the heat. After you wash the spinach, pop it in a salad spinner or use paper towel to remove the excess dampness.

When the pumpkin is done, I like to pop the wedges on a grill skillet over high heat to put some char marks on it for two reasons. Reason number one: it caramelises and adds to the taste. Reason number two: it looks super hot!

Place the spinach and half the balsamic glaze in a large bowl and toss to coat. Add the pumpkin, pine nuts and the rest of the balsamic glaze. Transfer a portion directly into the lunchbox.

TIPS

Make a double batch of this for dinner so that you have leftovers for lunch the next day.

I like to add goat's cheese when I make this for myself. Alternatively, you can add grilled chicken for extra protein; just make sure it's refrigerated well when packing a school lunch.

Gluten free
To make this recipe gluten free, use gluten-free balsamic glaze.

Vegan
Replace the honey with maple syrup to make this salad vegan.

GRISSINI ROLL-UPS

These are bloody awesome: they look and taste fantastic, contain the grains, dairy and protein your kids need and fit perfectly into school lunchboxes. I came up with a genius way of creating glue, but more on that a little later. Let's do this.

1 tablespoon camembert or brie, at room temperature

6 grissini sticks

6 slices of ham

6 slices of havarti or Swiss cheese

Makes 6

NF EF

Just a quick heads up – you will be using a pinch of the inside goopy bit of the camembert or brie as glue, so be prepared to get a little sticky. It needs to be at room temperature, so grab it out of the fridge before you start.

Ideally, the grissini should be around 10 cm long, so you might have to cut them down to size.

Square up the ham a little with a knife to give it more of a rectangular shape. Cut the cheese into pieces that are roughly the same size as the ham.

Roll the ham around the grissini nice and tight. Now roll the cheese around the ham and when you get to the end put a little of the sticky camembert or brie on the edge of the cheese and push down so that it sticks. Genuis, right?

I like to do three grissini like this and three where I switch the order of the ham and cheese so you get a couple of different types of roll-ups in the lunchbox.

TIP
Let the camembert or brie sit at room temperature for at least 30 minutes before using for the perfect goopy glue consistency.

Gluten free
Gluten-free grissini are available at health-food stores.

Vego
Use plant-based ham.

KIKI'S SHOPSKA SALATA
(MACEDONIAN CHOPPED SALAD)

This is my daughter Kiki's version of the Macedonian hit salad, shopska salata. The traditional version uses brown onion, but Kiki prefers red onion.

200 g (1 cup) quartered cherry tomatoes

1 cucumber, diced

¼ red onion, finely chopped

pinch of sea salt

3 tablespoons extra-virgin olive oil

1 tablespoon white vinegar

150 g (1 cup) crumbled feta

Serves 2–4

GF NF EF V

When Kiki makes this salad she insists on absolutely no help at all. It's not always perfect, but the taste is always amazingly awesome.

According to Kiki, there's no right or wrong way to construct this salad — sometimes she mixes the feta through the whole salad, other times she mixes the other ingredients together then puts it on top.

TIP

Kiki makes this directly into her lunchbox (she hates cleaning up).

Dairy free/vegan

Use your favourite vegan feta or even diced avocado in place of the regular feta.

Fussy eaters

Mild cheese like bocconcini would work instead of the feta. Omit the onion if the flavour is too strong.

CHEESEBURGER SKEWERS

**These cheeseburger skewers are pretty much all about the assembly.
You'll need three of my Italian meatballs for this recipe. Let's go.**

3 brioche hamburger buns

6 small wooden skewers

3 cooked Italian Meatballs
(see page 62), halved

3 slices of cheddar, each cut
into 4 squares

3 dill pickles, finely sliced

SPECIAL SAUCE

2 tablespoons mayonnaise

1 teaspoon mustard

1 teaspoon tomato sauce

1 teaspoon finely chopped
red onion

Makes 6

NF

Let's create the special sauce. Mix all the ingredients in a cup or small mixing bowl.

Use a small cookie cutter or espresso cup to cut a couple of circles from each brioche bun. Now use a bread knife to cut the bun circles horizontally to create mini brioche hamburger buns. Spread a teaspoon of the special sauce on the base of each mini brioche bun.

Thread a mini brioche base onto a skewer followed by pickles, cheese and half a meatball. Continue the layering with another piece of brioche bun, pickles, cheese and half a meatball. Finally, thread on a mini brioche bun lid. Repeat to make six skewers.

Pop into the lunchbox with an airtight container of special sauce for extra dipping, if you like.

TIP

Be sure to snip the points off the wooden skewers with some scissors so that the little peeps don't accidentally stab anyone with them.

Gluten free
Use gluten-free breadcrumbs in the Italian meatballs and gluten-free buns.

Dairy free
Opt for plant-based parmesan in the meatballs and use plant-based cheese slices instead of the cheddar.

Vego/vegan
Use my no-meat balls (see page 73) instead of the Italian meatballs to make these vego. For vegan, also sub in plant-based cheese and egg-free mayo.

Extra veg
Slide halved cherry tomatoes onto the skewers to add a bit of colourful veg. Replace the pickles with fresh cucumber slices if your kids prefer.

There are so many ways to fill baked cobb loaves (see page 40) and they are great for hiding diced veg in the base.

Head to page 85 to learn how to make these fun grissini roll-ups.

GARDEN SALAD SURPRISE

Originally I made this salad using leftovers, but over time my daughter Kiki and I have tweaked it and it has become a next-level salad. Are you intrigued? Check out the recipe and be blown away.

1 teaspoon extra-virgin olive oil

1 garlic clove, finely chopped

20 g butter

2 dinner rolls, sliced into quarters lengthways (they will look like little cigars)

8 slices of prosciutto

½ iceberg or cos lettuce, chopped

75 g (½ cup) cherry tomatoes, halved or quartered

½ cucumber, finely sliced into rounds

¼ red onion, finely sliced

75 g (½ cup) bocconcini, torn

125 ml (½ cup) store-bought Italian dressing

Serves 4

NF EF

Before you start frying, line a large plate with paper towel.

Grab your frying pan, add the oil and warm it over low heat. Add the garlic: we want it to sweat but not crisp, so focus Daniel-san – low heat is the key here. A couple of minutes should do.

Add the butter and wait for it to melt, then drop in the bread pieces and jiggle the pan to coat the bread in the garlic and butter. Continue to cook for around 1 minute on low heat, tossing the pan so that the croutons toast evenly. When the croutons are nice and golden on all sides, set them aside on the paper towel. Allow the croutons to cool a little (to avoid burning your fingers) before wrapping a slice of prosciutto around each crouton.

Reheat the same pan over low heat, then drop in the prosciutto bundles to lightly crisp. This will take around 2 minutes, turning the bundles as necessary. Is your mouth watering yet? Mine is and I need to clean the dribble off the keyboard. Lol.

Place all the veggies in a salad bowl, then add the bocconcini and dressing and give it a good toss. Drop in the prosciutto croutons and serve straight into the lunchbox.

Gluten free
Use crispy chickpeas or toasted seeds instead of the croutons for some crunch. If you choose this option, simply dice the prosciutto.

Dairy free
Use plant-based butter and bocconcini.

Vego/vegan
For a vegetarian option, omit the prosciutto and add extra bocconcini or a second cheese such as feta. For vegan, also sub in plant-based butter and cheese.

JAFFLES
AND MELTS

POSTIES

This is my potato toastie: no bread required. Microwaved potatoes are used to create a brilliant take on a toastie, which I've renamed the postie! Warning: the smell of these is next level.

2 large potatoes (any variety is fine), unpeeled, quartered

60 g (½ cup) grated cheddar

½ green capsicum, diced

80 g (½ cup) diced salami

pinch of salt flakes

1 teaspoon smoked paprika

Makes 2

GF NF EF

Pop the potato in the microwave and cook on high for 8 minutes.

While your potato is in the microwave, fire up the jaffle maker or sandwich maker. You can even use a sausage roll maker for these.

After 8 minutes in the microwave, test your potato. It should be cooked through and mashable.

Place half the potato on the bottom of your hot jaffle or sandwich maker to create a base for each of the two posties. Use a fork to press down on the potato to roughly mash it and spread it evenly across the base. Top the potato with the cheese, capsicum, salami, salt and paprika. Place the remaining potato on top and again roughly mash with a fork and spread to create a top layer for your postie. Close the jaffle or sandwich maker lid and cook until the potato is nice and crispy and the cheese is melted – around 5–7 minutes.

Pop the posties in the lunchbox hot or cold and wait for them to be devoured.

TIPS

If you want the postie to be warm in the kids' lunchboxes, wrap the hot postie in foil.

You could add a small tub of ketchup as a dipping sauce to go with the postie.

Dairy free

Substitute the cheddar with plant-based cheddar.

Vego/vegan

Skip the salami and add extra diced vegetables. For vegan, also sub in plant-based cheese.

Extra veg

Add some thinly sliced zucchini or mushroom inside the postie.

Fussy eaters

For a milder tasting postie, omit the salami and paprika.

Hawaiian pizza skewers for lunch? You betcha! Check out page 78 to learn how.

Your kids will love these panko-crumbed tuna balls (see page 58). Just add some fresh fruit and veg and lunch is sorted.

CUBAN SALADA MELTS

This might sound crazy, but it's bloody good – it almost has a crunchy pizza vibe. There are no rules when it comes to the toppings, but I'm going to share my classic Cubano (I've swapped out the roast pork for roast chicken). Let's do this.

8 Salada biscuits

8 slices of Swiss cheese

350 g (2 cups) shredded chicken (see page 37 for a recipe)

4 slices of ham

1 tablespoon mustard

4 dill pickles, sliced lengthways

Makes 4

NF EF

Preheat the oven grill to 240°C and line a baking tray with baking paper.

Place the Saladas on the baking tray (if none of your Saladas are cracked, chipped or broken you are the chosen one). Okay, so now pop a slice of cheese onto each Salada and put the tray in the oven. All you need is for the cheese to melt, which will take around 3 minutes – personally, I like a little golden brown kiss on the cheese, but each to their own. When you have melted the cheese to your satisfaction, remove the tray from the oven.

Remember that we are making four sandwiches – or as I call them Saladawiches – so we are only loading up four; the other four are the lids. Add the shredded chicken, then the ham. Smear some mustard on the ham then add your sliced pickles. Pop on the cheesy lids. You'll find that the cheese from the top Salada will melt over the ingredients. This is a big yes!

Let the Salada melts cool before adding them to the lunchbox.

Gluten free

Ditch the Saladas and use gluten-free bread slices or crackers as your base.

Dairy free

Plant-based cheese is a great substitute here – go for plant-based mozzarella as it melts nicely.

Vego/vegan

Turn this into a vego stack by using roasted eggplant and smoked paprika in place of the meat. For vegan, also sub in plant-based cheese.

BLACK BEAN & CAPSICUM QUESADILLAS

What do I love most about these quesadillas? (Apart from saying 'quesadillas' in a Mexican accent.) You can fill them with goodies or use them to dip into something delicious. Either way, the secret is to always make sure the cheese is melted.

1 avocado, plus extra to serve (optional)

1 tablespoon extra-virgin olive oil

½ brown onion, finely chopped

½ red capsicum, finely sliced

400 g can black beans, drained and rinsed

pinch of sea salt

1 teaspoon smoked paprika

2 large flatbreads or tortillas (flour and corn both work)

juice from ½ lime

60 g (½ cup) grated cheddar

Serves 4

NF EF V

First, mash the avo in a bowl. I find a fork is the way to go.

Heat the oil in a frying pan over medium heat. Add the onion and cook for 3 minutes, then add the capsicum and cook for 2 minutes more, stirring occasionally. Now stir in the black beans, salt and paprika. Cook for 3–4 minutes, or until the beans have heated up and the capsicum has softened. Transfer to a bowl.

Wipe out the pan and put it back over the heat. Place a flatbread in the pan and heat for 30 seconds on each side.

Now it's time to assemble. Add half the bean mixture to one half of a flatbread, then top with half the avocado, lime juice and cheese. Fold the flatbread in half so all the ingredients are covered, then pop it back into the pan over medium heat with the cheese side facing down. Cook for 2 minutes, or until the cheese has melted. Now flip the quesadilla over to heat the other side for around 1 minute. If it's looking a little too fat, squash it down with a spatula. Repeat this process to make the second quesadilla.

Cut the quesadillas in half and put them in the lunchbox with some extra avo, if desired. Wrap them in foil to keep them warm.

TIPS

You can make the black bean filling the night before, so that all you need to do in the morning is assemble and heat. The black beans will keep for 3–4 days in an airtight container in the fridge.

To make these even more delicious, you can also melt cheese on the outside of the quesadilla. Simply sprinkle some extra grated cheddar into the frying pan, then place the folded quesadilla into the pan on top of the cheese and cook as above.

Gluten free
There are plenty of gluten-free flatbread options to choose from or use corn tortillas.

Dairy free/vegan
Substitute the cheddar with a plant-based cheddar.

Fussy eaters
If your kids are not keen on capsicum, try chopping it super finely so that it disappears into the black bean mix.

SAVOURY WAFFLES

Waffles for lunch? Yep, that's what everyone says when I tell them I make my girls waffles for lunch. Waffles don't have to be full of sugar or covered in maple syrup and ice cream. I love making these savoury waffles because they're a great alternative to bread and are super easy to whip up. I use a heart-shaped waffle maker, which adds to the fun.

½ red capsicum, finely chopped

½ yellow capsicum, finely chopped

2 tablespoons finely chopped brown onion

60 g (½ cup) grated cheddar

WAFFLE BATTER

150 g (1 cup) self-raising flour

250 ml (1 cup) milk

20 g salted butter, melted

1 egg

pinch of sea salt

Makes 4

NF V

Turn on the waffle maker so that it heats up while you are preparing the waffle batter.

Use a handheld blender or a protein shaker to mix all the waffle batter ingredients till they're combined and almost thickshake like. Set aside.

The waffle maker should be ready to go now, so add in the capsicum and onion and let them soften and sweat until they start to get a little colour, around 2–3 minutes. Now add the cheese and let it melt a little, around 1 minute. Once you feel the vibe, pour the waffle batter on top of the cheese and veggies, being careful not to overfill. Close the lid of the waffle maker and cook for around 3 minutes, or until they're crispy and lightly golden.

Remember that these are super hot and need to cool down a little before you let your kids get to them. They look awesome in the lunchbox and are a great way to sneak in veggies. They can be served warm or cold.

TIPS

If you want these to be warm in the kids' lunchboxes, wrap the hot waffles in foil.

The batter for the waffles can be made the night before, however add an additional tablespoon of milk to the mix so it doesn't become too thick overnight in the fridge.

Gluten free
Use gluten-free self-raising flour.

Dairy free
Sub in plant-based cheddar, milk and butter.

Fussy eaters
Feel free to adapt the veggies to suit your small person's tastes.

NACHO BENTO

Nachos are a fun food: they're crunchy, they're gooey and kids love the idea of eating chips for a meal because they think they're pulling one over on us. Well, I figured out a way to outsmart my little humans by creating a nacho bento that is healthy, fun and super easy to make. Let's go amigos.

2 flatbreads

125 g (1 cup) grated cheddar

1 avocado

¼ red onion, finely diced

100 g (½ cup) diced tomatoes

⅓ cup coriander leaves, chopped (optional)

pinch of sea salt

1 tablespoon extra-virgin olive oil

3 tablespoons natural yoghurt

Serves 2

NF EF V

You can cook these in an air fryer or the oven. If cooking in the oven, preheat to 180°C fan-forced. Line a baking tray with baking paper. (Some air fryers won't fit two flatbreads side by side so the oven might be the way to go.)

Pop the flatbreads on the baking tray and place them in the oven or air fryer to crisp up on one side, around 2–3 minutes. Once they're lightly toasted on one side, take them out and flip them over. Sprinkle the cheese evenly over the flatbreads, keeping around 1 cm clear from the edge. Now pop them straight back into the oven or air fryer and bake for 2–3 minutes more, until the cheese is nicely melted (almost blistering). Let the flatbreads cool on the tray.

Cut the avocado in half and take out the stone. Scoop the avo flesh into a bowl but keep the shell intact as we will be reusing it a little later. Add all the remaining ingredients except the yoghurt to the bowl and gently mix with a fork to keep it chunky. Refill both the avo shells with the mixture. (There is always a little left over – this is for you to enjoy. You're welcome.)

Slice the cheesy flatbreads into triangles to create awesome nacho scoopers. Pop the avo halves into the lunchboxes with the cheesy triangles. Divide the yoghurt among tubs for dipping. You have officially become a nacho genius.

Gluten free
Choose gluten-free flatbreads or corn tortillas.

Dairy free/vegan
Substitute the cheddar with plant-based cheddar and use plant-based yoghurt for dipping.

Extra veg
Serve with some carrot and cucumber sticks for your kids to dip into any leftover avocado mixture.

Fussy eaters
Leave out the onion if you think this will be a deal breaker. You can also omit the coriander or swap it for any other herb or even baby spinach leaves, which have a mild flavour.

Super cheesy black bean quesadillas (see page 102) are an insanely delicious way to fill the lunchbox.

Lunchtime just got a bit more exciting with this eggsellent fried rice (see page 132). You can mix and match with whatever veggies and meat your little peeps are into.

MOREISH HALOUMI CANNOLI

Puff pastry to the rescue! The beauty of making these the night before is that the pressure is off in the morning. I recommend making a few extra as you won't be able to go to bed without eating a couple.

1 sheet of frozen puff pastry, just thawed

180 g haloumi

6 slices of prosciutto

1 egg, whisked

1 teaspoon sesame seeds

Makes 6

NF

You can cook these cannoli in an air fryer or the oven. If you are cooking in the oven, preheat to 180°C fan-forced. Line a baking tray with baking paper.

Cut the pastry sheet into six rectangles. Slice the haloumi into six rectangles around the same length as the pastry rectangles.

To make the cannoli, place a rectangle of puff pastry on your benchtop. Now place the prosciutto, then the haloumi on top of the pastry. Carefully wrap the pastry around the haloumi and prosciutto. Press the two edges of the pastry together to seal.

Repeat to make all the cannoli and place them on the baking tray.

Brush the cannoli with the egg and sprinkle the sesame seeds on top. Pop them in the oven for 10–12 minutes, or until golden brown and the haloumi is oozing. If using an air fryer, cook at 180°C for 12 minutes.

Leave to cool slightly before popping into the lunchbox.

TIPS

These are an occasional food. Add a little salad on the side for extra points.

FYI, these cannoli make terrific finger food for parties. If you want to take them in a sweet direction, drizzle with a little honey after you've taken them out of the oven.

Soaking the haloumi in water for 5–10 minutes before using reduces the saltiness of the cheese.

Gluten free

Use gluten-free puff pastry, which is readily available in supermarkets.

Egg free

Replace the egg wash with your milk of choice to brush over the cannoli.

Vego

Omit the prosciutto or replace it with asparagus to make these vegetarian.

GOLD-CLASS LUNCHES

MINI ROAST CHICKEN TACOS

Tacos are always awesome. And this lunchbox regular makes them even awesomer! They're great on a platter at a kid's party too (and when I say kids, I mean those aged between three and 83).

2 flatbreads or tortillas

1 teaspoon smoked paprika

60 g (½ cup) grated cheddar

½ avocado, finely sliced

½ tomato, finely sliced

90 g (½ cup) shredded roast chicken (see page 37 for a recipe)

3 tablespoons natural yoghurt

small handful of coriander leaves (optional)

½ lime

Makes 8–10

NF EF

You can cook these tacos in an air fryer or the oven. If cooking in the oven, preheat to 180°C fan-forced. Time to get the muffin tray from the cupboard and turn it upside down.

Use a round cookie cutter or a glass to cut four or five circles from each flatbread or tortilla. Fold them into a taco shape, place them in the valleys of the muffin tray and sprinkle with the smoked paprika. Smart, hey?

Pop the tray in the oven for about 8 minutes — you just want the shells to harden up enough that they maintain their shape. Take them out of the oven and let them cool down. If using an air fryer, cook at 180°C for 4–5 minutes.

Okay, now comes the assembly. Divide the cheese among the mini tacos, then add the avo, tomato, chicken, a dollop of yoghurt and a coriander leaf (if using). To finish off, squeeze a little lime juice on top.

Place the mini tacos side by side in the lunchbox so they fit nice and snug. Pack the lunchbox inside a cooler bag with an ice block to keep the temp of the chicken below 4°C.

Gluten free	Dairy free	Vego/vegan	Fussy eaters
Gluten-free flatbreads are always a great sub for standard flatbreads, or use corn tortillas.	Substitute the cheddar with plant-based cheddar and use plant-based yoghurt.	You can always swap out the chicken for beans — a Mexican 3-bean mix would work well. Also sub in plant-based cheese and yoghurt for vegan.	Let your kids assemble their own taco to give them a sense of 'I made my own lunch' — this worked a treat for my former fussy little human.

MAC 'N' CHEESE, YES PLEASE!

Mac 'n' cheese is my daughter Anela's fave school lunch. Now that she's in high school and officially a big girl, I decided to introduce the thermos. Does it work? Hell yes! The key is to heat it before filling it with food (see Tips). This recipe is a quick and easy go-to, one that I can make fresh in the morning while I drink my coffee. For the record, this thermos always comes back empty – it's well worth a go.

500 ml (2 cups) milk

20 g salted butter

250 g dried pasta (we love small macaroni)

125 g (1 cup) grated cheddar

Serves 4

NF EF V

Bring the milk to a boil in a small saucepan and stir in the butter. When the butter has melted, add the pasta. Follow the packet instructions for cooking times – it's usually around 8–10 minutes. You'll have to stir every few minutes, okay? Don't forget.

Check that the pasta is cooked through by burning your mouth trying one, then turn off the heat. Most of the milk will be evaporated but drain any remaining. Sprinkle in the cheese and stir until the cheese melts and there is even coverage.

Transfer the mac 'n' cheese to a preheated thermos (see Tips) and quickly close the lid. Now all you do is wait till after school to hear the rave reviews. The only big pain in the butt is cleaning the dried cheese from inside the thermos – but it's worth it.

TIPS

If your kids are adventurous, you can spice it up a little by adding a sprinkle of smoked paprika.

To keep the food nice and hot fill a thermos with boiling water and close the lid so the internal lining of the stainless steel heats up. Let it sit for 10 minutes before replacing the hot water with the hot food.

Gluten free

There are a heap of awesome gluten-free pasta choices available from the supermarket.

Dairy free/vegan

For a dairy-free and vegan option, ditch the milk for water or plant-based milk and sub in dairy-free butter and cheese. I recommend dairy-free grated parmesan but only use half the amount as it's a little bitey. Add the parmesan while on low heat.

Extra veg

Add 1 cup of cauliflower florets to the pasta with 3 minutes of cooking time left. Drain with the pasta and continue with the recipe as above.

Fill a thermos with creamy mac 'n' cheese (see page 116), add some freshness on the side and lunch is done.

These avocado pastry cups (see page 131) are easy to make and a super fancy lunchbox addition.

VEGETABLE OODLES OF NOODLES

I make this at least once a week for my daughters (it's also made its way to our dinner table a few times). This recipe always changes when I make it: I use whatever veggies I have – sometimes there's capsicum in it and sometimes there's a load of cauliflower. The hardest part is not taking it to work for your own lunch and giving the kids a lunch order. Good luck.

2 x 72 g packets of 2-minute noodles

1 tablespoon vegetable oil

½ red capsicum, finely sliced

1 small carrot, cut into matchsticks

30 g (½ cup) small broccoli florets

60 g (½ cup) small cauliflower florets

3 teaspoons soy sauce

80 g (1 cup) sugar snap peas, halved lengthways

Serves 2–3

NF DF EF VG

Gluten free

To make this recipe gluten free, swap the 2-minute noodles for rice noodles (I like the 'just add hot water' kind as they're easy and quick) and choose a gluten-free soy sauce or swap it out for another gluten-free sauce, such as Marion's Kitchen Honey Soy.

Crank up the kettle.

Drop the 2-minute noodles in a small saucepan, then pour in enough boiling water to cover the noodles. Whack the lid on top.

Now grab a wok or frying pan and heat the oil over medium heat. Drop in the veggies except the sugar snap peas – we want those to remain crunchy. Cook for around 3–4 minutes, until the veg starts sweating a little.

After 2 minutes the noodles should be ready … if they're not, I've been living a lie my whole life. Anyway, drain the noodles and drop them into the wok, add the soy sauce and mix it all up (I find using tongs works best). Once the noodles are glistening with the soy sauce – around 30–60 seconds – turn off the heat, add the sugar snap peas and give everything one final toss.

Add the noodles straight into preheated thermoses (see Tips) and quickly close the lids. The idea of not cooking the sugar snap peas is to retain their beautiful crunch and, according to my daughter Kiki, the pop of the peas is a heap of fun.

TIPS

Cook up some finely sliced beef strips before you cook the veggies to make it a beef and veggie noodle delight. Add any protein you like – even tofu if it woks your taste buds.

To keep the food nice and hot, fill a thermos with boiling water and close the lid so the internal lining of the stainless steel heats up. Let it sit for 10 minutes before replacing the hot water with the hot food.

You can chop the veggies the night before and pop them in an airtight container in the fridge to save time.

EASIEST CRUMPETS EVER

Crumpets are pretty cool. When I make these, the toppings always change: sometimes I make sweet ones with the traditional strawberry jam, sometimes it's melted cheese and crispy bacon. Use whatever you have in the fridge to make these your own.

½ teaspoon sea salt

150 g (1 cup) self-raising flour

180 ml (¾ cup) warm water

2 teaspoons caster sugar

7 g sachet of instant dried yeast

20 g salted butter

Makes 4

NF EF V

Pop all the ingredients except the butter in a protein shaker — if you don't have a protein shaker you can simply use a whisk. Ideally, put the salt in first and then add the yeast last — we separate these two ingredients so that the salt doesn't stop the fermentation process. Shake the shaker (or whisk the whisk) really well, almost like being at a Rage Against the Machine concert and they're playing 'Killing In The Name'. After a few minutes you can stop. Now pop the protein shaker aside for 15–20 minutes, we want the yeast to do its thing.

Grab four cookie cutters or egg rings and grease them well.

Warm a shallow frying pan over medium heat, then add the butter and let it melt. Pop the cookie cutters or egg rings in the frying pan and pour in the mixture until it reaches halfway up the sides. When the mixture has set a little — around 60–90 seconds — remove the cutters or rings using a small cake spatula and flip the crumpets over. Cook for another minute or two. We want them to be a little golden but not out of control burnt-toast style. If you feel they're cooking too fast, lower the heat.

The best way to know if they're cooked is to stick a skewer in them — if the skewer is sticky it means they're not ready.

Once cooked, add your favourite toppings. I like to cut the crumpets in half to create a sandwich vibe, then I add cheese, crispy bacon, avocado and tomato. Delicious and perfect for the lunchbox!

Dairy free/vegan
Replace the butter with Nuttelex or extra-virgin olive oil to make dairy-free and vegan crumpets.

Extra veg
Halve the crumpets and turn them into little salad sandwiches, with grated carrot, cucumber, tomato, lettuce and a slice of cheese.

CAN'T DENY THIS STIR-FRY

My good friend Alex owns my favourite Chinese restaurant in Geelong and he taught me that day-old steamed rice works best in stir-fries. You can use any veggies your little people like in this recipe. My youngest, Kiki, loves adding a squeeze of lime for freshness.

1 tablespoon vegetable oil

1 garlic clove, crushed

½ brown onion, finely chopped

300 g porterhouse steak, sliced into 1.5 cm thick strips

3 teaspoons soy sauce

3 teaspoons oyster sauce

1 carrot, cut into matchsticks

1 red capsicum, thinly sliced

30 g (½ cup) broccoli florets

60 g (½ cup) cauliflower florets

100 g (1 cup) snow peas, trimmed

185 g (1 cup) steamed rice

Serves 4

NF DF EF

Heat the vegetable oil in a wok or frying pan over medium heat. Add the garlic and onion and cook for 2 minutes to soften. Once the onion starts to become translucent, add the steak and stir. Cook for around 1–2 minutes – as soon as the steak starts to sear, add the sauces, followed by the veggies. Cook for 2–3 minutes, then remove from the heat. Remember, the thermos will continue to cook the food till lunchtime, so don't stress if you think the veggies or protein are a little undercooked.

Heat a cup of steamed rice in the microwave till it's scorching hot, about 90 seconds should do it. Add it to the base of preheated thermoses (see Tips), then add the stir-fry. Remember to pour in the sauce that's left in the wok or pan as the rice will absorb it all. Pop on the thermos lids and you're good to go.

TIPS

You can prepare this meal the night before. You could even batch-cook this recipe and freeze portions for up to 3 months.

You can use chicken instead of beef, but make sure the chicken is cooked right through before you pop it in the thermos and use the brown part of the chicken as the breast will dry up a little.

To keep the food nice and hot, fill a thermos with boiling water and close the lid so the internal lining of the stainless steel heats up. Let it sit for 10 minutes before replacing the hot water with the hot food.

Gluten free
Choose gluten-free soy and oyster sauces.

Vegan
To make this vegan, replace the oyster sauce with mushroom stir-fry sauce and the steak with strips of tofu.

MINI BEEF SLIDERS

Mini beef sliders are everything that lunchbox food should be: bite sized, fun and delicious. When I initially made these for my girls, I didn't expect just how much they would love the novelty of having burgers for lunch. I decided to make them as healthy as possible while maintaining their super cuteness. These are a winner and they also make great party food.

4 x mini burger buns, halved

4 x cooked No-Fuss Beef Patties (see page 53)

4 slices of cheddar

4 lettuce leaves (any lettuce is fine)

1 tomato, finely sliced

1 dill pickle, finely sliced

BIG G SAUCE

2 tablespoons mayonnaise

1 tablespoon tomato sauce

1 tablespoon American mustard

½ teaspoon onion powder

½ teaspoon garlic powder

1 teaspoon white vinegar

Makes 4

NF

To make the sauce, place all the ingredients in a small bowl and whisk until the ingredients are combined.

These sliders are really simple to assemble. Add a dollop of the sauce on the base of each bun, then add a burger patty to each, followed by a slice of cheese, a lettuce leaf, a slice of tomato and a few slices of pickle. Finish with another dollop of the sauce and the top of the bun. You can insert a skewer to keep everything together, if you like.

Transfer to the lunchbox and you're good to go.

TIP

Pop a toothpick through the sliders if you want to make extra sure they stay together in the lunchbox. Remember to cut off the pointy end!

Gluten free	Dairy free	Vego/vegan	Extra veg
Use gluten-free rolls and gluten-free breadcrumbs in the beef patties.	Sub in plant-based cheddar.	Use my no-meat balls (see page 73) to make these vegetarian. For vegan, also sub in plant-based cheese and egg-free mayo.	Add grated carrot and canned beetroot slices to up the veg in these sliders.

Turn your leftover beef patties (see page 53) into these delicious sliders (see page 126). They can be whipped up in a matter of minutes!

There's no better way to eat your veg than this! Head to page 120 for my vegetable oodles of noodles recipe.

FRESH AVOCADO PASTRY CUPS

When I make these, I like to imagine they're the kind of thing you'd find in a French patisserie in Mexico. I guess my mind is a little bit unusual. In any case, I thought these were a great way to combine the two food cultures.

4 sheets of filo pastry, just thawed if frozen

40 g salted butter, melted

2 avocados

3 slices of cheddar

2 roma tomatoes, finely sliced

6 cherry tomatoes, halved

Makes 6

NF EF V

You can cook these pastry cups in an air fryer or the oven. If cooking in the oven, preheat to 180°C fan-forced. Grab a nonstick muffin tray with at least six muffin holes.

Stack the pastry sheets on top of one another, brushing melted butter between each layer as you go. Cut the filo into six even squares (please don't get a ruler — close enough is good enough). Place the squares in the middle of the muffin holes and push them down so that they contour to the sides. Drizzle melted butter over the bases and sides of the pastry cups. Place the tray in the oven and cook the pastry cups for 6–8 minutes, or until they turn nice and golden — you want a similar colour to a croissant. If using an air fryer, cook at 180°C for 5 minutes.

In the meantime, scoop the avocado flesh into a ziplock bag, expel as much air as possible and seal the seam. Bash the avo around a little, until it is mashed and there are no big bits. We are going to use the ziplock bag as a piping bag, so stand by.

Allow the pastry cups to cool down, then remove them from the muffin tray — they should look like flower cups just waiting to be filled.

First up, use a small cookie cutter to cut two perfect circles from each slice of cheddar. Place a slice of cheese into the base of each pastry cup. Now snip the corner off the ziplock bag and pipe 2 cm of smashed avocado into each cup. Add a slice or two of tomato and finish off with a dollop of smashed avocado and a cherry tomato on top — it almost looks like a cupcake! Enjoy.

Dairy free/vegan
Use dairy-free butter and plant-based cheese.

Fussy eaters
The avocado can be swapped out for yoghurt, hummus or any dip your little peeps would prefer.

EGGSELLENT FRIED RICE

I had to include this recipe in the book: as a dad I've been dying to use the term 'eggsellent' for a long time. So here it is. The key is to ensure you have steamed rice in the fridge from the night before. Let's get cracking ... get it, cracking the eggs.

1 tablespoon vegetable oil

½ brown onion, finely chopped

2 garlic cloves, crushed

2 cups mixed veggies (sweetcorn, sugar snap peas, broccoli, carrot, zucchini, cauliflower), cut into 1 cm pieces

2 eggs

185 g (1 cup) steamed rice

2 tablespoons soy sauce

coriander leaves, to serve (optional)

Serves 2–4

NF DF V

If you have a wok, you rock! If not, grab a frying pan.

Heat the vegetable oil in the wok or pan over high heat, then add the onion and garlic and stir for 2 minutes – or just wait for the delicious smell to hit you. Add the veggies and cook for a further 3 minutes to soften up a little. Now add the eggs and keep stirring for around 90 seconds – you want the eggs to break up once cooked. Add the rice and soy sauce and cook like they do in the Chinese noodle shop: you want to get the rice nice and hot – it will break up nicely once it heats up.

The cooking time is fast with this dish, so stay focused and be sure to have your hot thermos ready to go (see Tips).

Garnish with coriander if your little peeps are into it.

TIPS

Adding beef, pork, chicken or prawns is always a winning idea; you can even add cooked pineapple for a summery vibe.

To keep the fried rice nice and hot, fill a thermos with boiling water and close the lid so the internal lining of the stainless steel heats up. Let it sit for 10 minutes before replacing the hot water with the hot food.

Gluten free
Use gluten-free soy sauce.

Egg free/vegan
Simply omit the eggs and it will still be absolutely delicious.

Fussy eaters
You can replace the brown onion with red onion as the flavour isn't as strong, or just leave it out entirely. Skip the coriander if it's likely to offend!

LIFE-SAVING LUNCHBOX BAKES

VEGETARIAN FRITTATA BAKE

These frittata slices freeze really well and are perfect for batch cooking. This recipe enables you to get creative with a heap of veggies, so get ready to tap into your inner artist.

10 eggs

250 ml (1 cup) thickened cream

1 teaspoon sea salt

1 tablespoon dried oregano

125 g (1 cup) grated cheddar

150 g (1 cup) crumbled feta

1 large mushroom, finely sliced

1 zucchini, finely sliced

½ red capsicum, finely sliced

½ green capsicum, finely sliced

½ yellow capsicum, finely sliced

150 g (¾ cup) tiny tom tomatoes

1 tablespoon extra-virgin olive oil

Serves 8–10

NF GF V

You can cook the frittata in an air fryer or the oven. If cooking in the oven, preheat to 180°C fan-forced. Line a large rectangular baking dish (roughly 30 cm x 22 cm) with baking paper.

Grab a large mixing bowl and have fun cracking in the eggs – this is where I practise my one-handed egg cracking. Use a whisk to lightly mix in the cream, salt and oregano until it just becomes creamy (not over-the-top soufflé creamy).

Pour three-quarters of the egg mixture into the dish, then add half the cheddar and half the crumbled feta. Start decorating the dish with the veggies – you can assemble in colour order or even create a picture – be as creative as you want. You can drop the tiny tomatoes from a distance for some Salt Bae vibes. Slowly pour the remaining egg mixture on top of the veggies, then add the remaining cheeses. Drizzle the olive oil on top (especially over the mushroom). Turn your oven down to 165°C and pop the dish in. Bake for around 35 minutes – it will have a focaccia vibe when done. If using an air fryer, cook at 160°C for 20–22 minutes.

Allow the frittata to cool in the dish before slicing into eight or ten lunchbox portions.

TIP

This bake keeps well in an airtight container in the fridge for 5 days or frozen for up to 1 month. To defrost, place the frozen portions in the fridge the night before use.

Dairy free

Use dairy-free cream or yoghurt instead of the thickened cream, and plant-based cheddar and feta.

Fussy eaters

Adjust this recipe with any combination of your kid's favourite veggies to accommodate picky eaters.

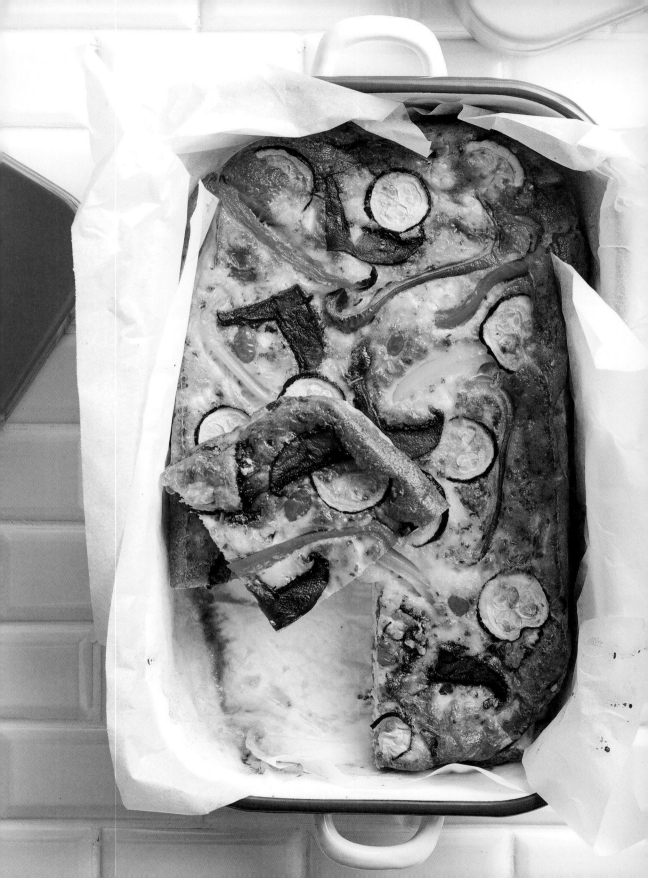

PIZZA BAGELS

If you don't have frozen puff pastry in your freezer, are we even friends? Just kidding. Seriously though, I have a pack of 10 in the freezer ready to go at all times. Right now, we're going to smash out some pizza bagels … fasten your seatbelts ladies and gentlemen.

1 sheet of frozen puff pastry, just thawed

90 g (⅓ cup) salt-free tomato paste

80 g (½ cup) shredded ham

40 g (¼ cup) pitted kalamata olives, sliced

10 basil leaves

150 g (1 cup) grated mozzarella

Makes 4

NF EF

You can cook these in an air fryer or the oven. If cooking in the oven, preheat to 180°C fan-forced. Line a baking tray with baking paper.

Slice the pastry sheet in half and then half again lengthways to get four long rectangles of pastry.

Smear the tomato paste evenly along the strips, leaving a 1 cm border around the edge. Add the ham, olives and basil leaves, then sprinkle the mozzarella on top.

Fold each rectangle in half lengthways to create a long strip. Roll one strip around your fingers to create a loose bagel shape. Press the end of the pastry in with your fingers to seal it. Repeat to make four bagels.

Pop the pizza bagels in the oven for 25 minutes. When done, they should be golden brown and puffed up. If using an air fryer, cook at 180°C for 15 minutes.

Allow to cool and place in the lunchbox.

TIPS

You can prepare these the night before, pop them in the fridge overnight and then bake in the morning. Once baked, they'll keep in an airtight container in the fridge for up to 2 days.

The unbaked bagels can also be frozen for up to 3 months. Allow to thaw before baking.

You can make a sweet version of these — jam and berries totally rock.

Gluten free

Use gluten-free puff pastry.

Dairy free

Use plant-based grated mozzarella and butter-free puff pastry.

Vego/vegan

For vego, use plant-based ham or bacon, or add capsicum slices instead. Also sub in plant-based mozzarella and butter-free puff pastry for vegan.

Extra veg

Add whatever veg your kids are into. Very thinly sliced zucchini, mushrooms, tomato or chopped spinach would all work well.

Fussy eaters

You can swap out the olives for pesto to suit fussy eaters.

SIMPLE VEGGIE MUFFINS

You can make this versatile recipe with any veggies you like to suit your kids. My girls love the melted cheese and veggies and always come back for more. This is a great little recipe that helps you clean out your fridge and pantry with veggies that are past their best.

1 egg

180 ml (¾ cup) milk

1 teaspoon sea salt

150 g (1 cup) self-raising flour

45 g (½ cup) cleaned, chopped mushroom

80 g (½ cup) chopped red capsicum

30 g (¼ cup) finely chopped spring onion

65 g cheddar, cut into 6 cubes

3 cherry tomatoes, halved

Makes 6

NF V

You can cook these muffins in an air fryer or the oven. If cooking in the oven, preheat to 180°C fan-forced. Line six holes of a nonstick muffin tray with paper cases.

Use a protein shaker or handheld blender to mix the egg, milk, salt and self-raising flour until the mixture is a thickshake consistency and all the ingredients are well combined.

Pour the mixture to a depth of 1 cm into the six paper cases. Distribute the mushroom, capsicum and spring onion evenly among the muffins, top each with a cube of cheese, then pour in the remaining mixture, stopping 1 cm from the top. Place half a cherry tomato on top of each muffin.

Bake the muffins for 20 minutes in the oven, until golden brown. Insert a skewer into the centre of a muffin to check — if it comes out clean they are good to go. If using an air fryer, cook at 180°C for 15 minutes.

Let the muffins cool down a little before you attempt to take them out of the tray.

TIP

Batch baking these muffins makes life easier in the mornings. Store the muffins in an airtight container in the pantry for 2–3 days or freeze for up to 1 month.

Gluten free
Use gluten-free self-raising flour.

Dairy free
Sub in your favourite plant-based milk and cheese.

Egg free/vegan
Replace the egg with any of the substitutes listed on page 26. For vegan, also sub in plant-based milk and cheese.

Fussy eaters
Change up the veg to suit your little peeps — grated carrot, sweet potato and pumpkin work well, as do peas and sweetcorn.

CHEESE & VEGEMITE TWISTIES

This is the final recipe I wrote for this book and I must say it was received amazingly well when the video went live — over 500K views in 24 hours! What I love about it is that it's as Aussie as it gets, with a modern twist.

1 sheet of frozen puff pastry, just thawed and cut into four squares

1 tablespoon Vegemite

150 g (1 cup) grated mozzarella

1 egg, whisked

1 tablespoon sesame seeds

Makes 4

NF V

You can cook these twisties in an air fryer or the oven. If cooking in the oven, preheat to 180°C fan-forced. Line a baking tray with baking paper.

Smear a teaspoon of Vegemite onto each pastry square, leaving a 1 cm border around the edge. Now evenly distribute the grated mozzarella among all four squares.

Time to get rolling. All we need to do is roll up each square of pastry — but not too tightly — so that they look like fat snakes. Working with one 'snake' at a time, grab one end with one hand and the other end with your other hand, and twist until you're happy with the look. Be careful not to over-twist as the pastry can rip. Repeat to make four twisties.

Place the twisties on the baking tray, brush with the egg wash and sprinkle over the sesame seeds. Bake for 20 minutes, until golden and crisp. If using an air fryer, cook at 180°C for 12 minutes.

Cool slightly before popping into the lunchbox.

TIP

These twisties can be made the night before, refrigerated overnight and baked in the morning. Once baked, store in an airtight container in the pantry, where they'll keep for up to 2 days.

Gluten free
Use gluten-free puff pastry.

Dairy free/vegan
For dairy free, use plant-based mozzarella and butter-free puff pastry. For vegan, also use 1 tablespoon of plant-based milk instead of the egg.

Egg free
Replace the egg wash with 1 tablespoon of your choice of milk.

These cheese and Vegemite twisties (see page 142) are sure to be devoured by the end of the school day.

I love pizza and I love bagels, so I decided to combine them. Introducing the pizza bagel (see page 138). You're welcome.

MEAT-LOVERS' FRITTATA

This frittata is for kids who love meat – and with the addition of potatoes this is a meat-and-chips kind of vibe. Get to know your local butcher and have a good look at the type of sausages they specialise in – I always ask for their specialty.

10 eggs

250 ml (1 cup) thickened cream

pinch of sea salt

1 cup grated potato

1 large mushroom, sliced

½ red capsicum, finely sliced

150 g (¾ cup) tiny tom tomatoes

225 g (1½ cups) crumbled feta or goat's cheese

1 cup finely sliced chorizo (about 1 cm thick)

1 cup finely sliced bacon

1 cup finely sliced pepperoni (about 3 mm thick)

2 tablespoons honey

1 tablespoon extra-virgin olive oil

Serves 8–10

NF GF

You can cook this frittata in an air fryer or the oven. If cooking in the oven, preheat to 180°C fan-forced. Line a 25 cm round baking dish with baking paper.

Crack the eggs into a mixing bowl, then add the cream and salt. Use a whisk to briefly mix until it just becomes creamy.

Pour the egg mixture into the baking dish, then top with the veggies and cheese. Scatter over the chorizo, bacon and pepperoni. (There are no rules about how to arrange the ingredients, but it's nice to evenly spread them out as the frittata will be cut into slices and this will ensure everyone gets a share of the ingredients.) For the grand finale, drizzle the honey on top and then the olive oil.

Turn your oven down to 160°C and pop the dish in. Bake the frittata for 40 minutes, or until it's a sizzling golden brown work of art. If using an air fryer, cook at 160°C for 28–30 minutes.

Allow the frittata to cool in the dish before slicing into eight or ten lunchbox portions.

TIP

This frittata keeps well in an airtight container in the fridge for 4 days or frozen for up to 1 month. To defrost, place the frozen portions in the fridge the night before use.

Dairy free
Use plant-based cream and cheese.

Fussy eaters
You can mix and match the veggies to suit your picky eater.

THREE-INGREDIENT SCONES

**Scones are so old-school that I had to make them cool for school.
Naturally, my daughters, Kiki and Anela, were my guinea pigs.
I regularly make these as a snack to sit in the pantry – you can be
slightly naughty and add jam and cream or you can easily swap out
the sweet stuff for savoury school-friendly toppings (see Tip).**

250 ml (1 cup) lemonade

250 ml (1 cup) thickened
cream

450 g (3 cups) self-raising
flour, plus extra for dusting

3 tablespoons milk

Makes 8–10

NF EF V

You can cook these in an air fryer or the oven. If cooking in
the oven, preheat to 170°C fan-forced. Line a baking tray with
baking paper.

Using a food processor for this recipe is controversial, as the
old-school way is to not overmix the ingredients. But rules were
made to be challenged, so here is my way.

Drop all the ingredients except the milk into a food processor
and blitz for 15 seconds only. Once the ingredients are combined,
take out the dough-like mixture and pop it on a flour-dusted
board. Push it down to make an even 2 cm thick dough, almost
like a pizza base.

Use a glass or an egg ring to cut circles out of the dough (I use
a 6 cm ring). Pop them on the baking tray. Gather the leftover
dough scraps, press them together and repeat the process.

Brush the milk on top of the scones and bake for 20–25 minutes.
The scones will be golden when ready and a skewer inserted into
the centre of a scone should come out clean. If using an air fryer,
cook at 170°C for 15–17 minutes – you might need to do them in
two batches, depending on the size of your air fryer.

Allow the scones to cool before placing in the lunchbox.

TIP

Be creative with the toppings – smoked salmon and cream cheese are
delicious on these scones, or a nut-free pesto with some ham, or even
just good old cheese.

Gluten free
Replace the self-raising flour with gluten-free
self-raising flour.

Dairy free/vegan
Use plant-based cream and milk.

These simple blueberry muffins (see page 156) will quickly become part of your lunchbox repertoire. Mix and match with different fruits to make them work for your child.

My crumpets (see page 123) work with all kinds of toppings, including the classic cheese and Vegemite.

NUT-FREE MUESLI CIRCLES

Having been caught out a few times when my girls had requested a mid-morning snack – 'but not fruit, Daaaaaad' – I knew it was time to hit them up with my style of muesli bar. This isn't an ordinary bar: it's a circle. Why? Because I wanted another use for my muffin trays. I think it's genius.

175 g (½ cup) honey

1 teaspoon vanilla extract

3 tablespoons melted coconut oil, plus 1 tablespoon extra for greasing

200 g (2 cups) rolled oats

30 g (⅓ cup) desiccated coconut

3 tablespoons pumpkin seeds

3 tablespoons finely chopped dried apple

2 tablespoons chia seeds

1 teaspoon ground cinnamon

Makes 6

NF DF EF V

You can cook these muesli circles in an air fryer or the oven. If cooking in the oven, preheat to 180°C fan-forced. Grab a muffin tray and a coffee – depending on the time of day. Grease the bases and sides of six muffin holes with the melted coconut oil.

Pour the honey, vanilla and coconut oil in a small mixing bowl and whisk together with a fork until combined. Place all the remaining ingredients in a large mixing bowl and briefly mix to combine. Add the wet ingredients to the dry and stir well, making sure the liquids combine well with the dry ingredients.

Divide the muesli mix among the six greased muffin holes and use a spoon or the base of a cup to push the mixture down so it's packed nice and tight. Whack the tray in the oven and cook for around 25 minutes, until golden brown. If using an air fryer, cook at 180°C for 15 minutes.

Let the muesli circles cool a little before taking them out of the tray and popping them into the lunchbox.

TIP

These muesli circles will keep in an airtight container in the pantry for up to 4 days.

Gluten free
Use gluten-free oats.

Vegan
Sub in maple syrup or rice malt syrup for the honey.

MANGO TURNOVERS

These sweet delights are super easy to make and don't have any added sugar. This recipe was invented one day when my girls wanted something sweet and all I had was a mango and frozen puff pastry. We've all heard about apple turnovers, so I thought I could make a mango turnover. The result was awesome and it's now become a regular lunchbox item.

1 mango

1 sheet of frozen puff pastry, just thawed and cut into four squares

seriously, that's all you need

Makes 4

NF EF V

You can cook these in an air fryer or the oven. If cooking in the oven, preheat to 180°C fan-forced. Line a baking tray with baking paper.

Peel the mango and slice it up.

Now we are going to score a section of each pastry square. On the right side of each square, score (being careful not to cut through the pastry) horizontal lines about 1 cm long from the middle of the pastry to the right of the pastry stopping 1 cm short of the edge. Score like this all the way from the top to the bottom of each square.

Now on the left, unscored side of the square, add the freshly cut mango and load it up. Fold the scored side over the mango and push it down along the edges. You can neaten up the edges by trimming them with a knife.

Cook the mango turnovers in the oven for 25 minutes, or until golden and the pastry has risen. If using an air fryer, cook at 180°C for 15 minutes.

The end result looks amazing, and these are awesome in the lunchbox or for an after-school snack. Enjoy!

TIP

This recipe can be used to create fruit turnovers with whatever lovely fruit you have to hand — apple is especially good.

Gluten free
Use gluten-free puff pastry.

Dairy free/vegan
Choose butter-free puff pastry.

GO-TO BLUEBERRY MUFFINS

This recipe is the perfect base to make any kind of sweet muffin for the lunchbox. All you need is a few simple ingredients and a muffin tray to make these delicious fruity muffins. I often change up the sweetener between maple syrup and honey, so choose the one that you have handy or you love the most.

1 egg

180 ml (¾ cup) milk

3 tablespoons honey or maple syrup, plus 1 tablespoon extra for drizzling (optional)

150 g (1 cup) self-raising flour

80 g (½ cup) fresh or frozen blueberries

Makes 6

NF V

You can cook these muffins in an air fryer or the oven. If cooking in the oven, preheat to 180°C fan-forced. Line six holes of a nonstick muffin tray with paper cases. (I've recently started to use paper cases in the muffin tray instead of butter to grease it – but go with whatever works for you.)

Use a protein shaker or handheld blender to mix the egg, milk, honey or maple syrup and self-raising flour until the mixture is a thickshake consistency and all the ingredients are well combined.

Pour the mixture into the six paper cases, stopping 1 cm from the top of each. Distribute the blueberries evenly among the muffins, pushing some in deeper and leaving some exposed.

Bake for 20–25 minutes in the oven, until the muffins are golden and cooked through. Insert a skewer into the centre of a muffin to check for doneness – if it comes out clean they are good to go. If using an air fryer, cook at 180°C for 15 minutes.

Allow the muffins to cool before taking them out of the muffin tray, as they're still a little fragile when warm. Finally, drizzle with a tablespoon of honey or maple syrup, if you like.

TIP

Store the muffins in an airtight container in the pantry for 2–3 days or freeze for up to 1 month.

Gluten free
Use gluten-free self-raising flour.

Dairy free
Use your favourite plant-based milk.

Egg free/vegan
Replace the egg with any of the substitutes listed on page 26. For vegan, also sub in plant-based milk and use maple syrup instead of honey.

Fussy eaters
Try swapping out the blueberries for apple and cinnamon or chocolate and banana. Raspberries and ½ teaspoon of lemon zest are a pretty awesome duo, too.

EASY NO-BAKE TREATS

CHOCOLATE PROTEIN BALLS

Goodness gracious, great balls of fire ... these are next-level. Throw away the lunchboxes because these are going straight down the hatch. Yep, trust me on this one. I've made these a dozen times and each time they're demolished. With that in mind, I recommend you make two batches. You'll thank me and so will the kids.

50 g (⅓ cup) unsalted macadamia nuts

150 g (1½ cups) quick oats

250 g (1 cup) almond butter

3 tablespoons chia seeds

2 tablespoons maple syrup

1 teaspoon vanilla extract

1 tablespoon cocoa powder, plus extra for rolling (optional)

Makes 15

DF EF VG

First, we need to smash the macadamia nuts into little pieces. The best way to do this is after you've asked the kids 100 times to do something and they still haven't done it – anger and stress release. Pop the macadamia nuts in a ziplock bag, expelling as much air as possible, and seal the seam. Cover the bag with a tea towel and bash the living daylights out of it till the nuts are crushed to your desired size (we don't want to make macadamia butter so chill out a little with the bashing).

Place the macadamias in a mixing bowl with all the remaining ingredients and stir until well combined.

Now it's time to get your hands dirty. Roll the balls to whatever size you like. (You can even make one massive ball so that when you eat it all you can comfortably say you only had one.) If the mixture is not quite holding together, add a touch more maple syrup.

Put some cocoa powder in a shallow bowl, then roll the balls in the cocoa to coat them. Transfer the balls to an airtight container and refrigerate.

TIPS

These will keep in an airtight container in the fridge for 4–5 days. They can also be stored in the freezer for up to 1 month.

Remember to make sure your school allows nuts before packing these in the lunchbox.

Gluten free
Simply use gluten-free oats and you're sorted!

Nut free
Swap the almond butter for tahini and the macadamias for pumpkin seeds or toasted buckwheat.

Fussy eaters
If your kids are not keen on the dusting of cocoa on the outside of these, roll them in desiccated coconut instead.

STRAWBERRY JAM CRUST ROLL-UPS

Of all the social media posts that I've done, this method of using up bread crusts has been the most popular and most shared. This recipe uses the same method but takes it to the next level to create roll-ups that are sweet, delicious and easy to make — they also look pretty awesome. Let's get rolling.

4 slices of bread

4 wooden skewers

20 g salted butter

2 tablespoons strawberry jam (or any jam you like)

Makes 4

NF EF V

Cut the crust off a slice of bread being sure to keep the crust intact in one continuous strip. Starting at one end, coil the crust up to look like a large snail, then pierce the crust with a skewer to keep it nice and tight. Repeat with the remaining slices of bread.

Heat a frying pan over medium–low heat, then add the butter. Once the butter melts, pop the roll-ups in and cook for around 2 minutes, flipping them over occasionally, until they get a nice toasty colour. Drop a teaspoon of jam on top of each roll-up then turn over and cook for 1 minute to caramelise and become almost toffee-like in texture. Do this on both sides of each roll-up.

When finished you can either leave the skewers in or take them out. Allow the roll-ups to cool before popping in the lunchbox.

TIPS

Remember to keep the skewers nearby when you roll up the crusts.

If you do leave the skewers in, be sure to snip the points off with some scissors so that the little peeps don't accidentally stab anyone with them.

Gluten free

Gluten-free bread works a treat in this recipe.

Dairy free/vegan

Swap out the butter for vegetable oil or dairy-free butter (choose one with coconut or olive oil for a palm oil–free option).

Savoury muffins (see page 141) are a lunchbox staple. You can whip them up in no time using a protein shaker or blender and can include whatever veggies your child is into.

These pistachio baklava balls (see page 170) are a pretty special treat for the lunchbox, and so easy to make.

DATE & ALMOND BLISS BALLS

These healthy energy balls are perfect for a mid-morning snack —
and pure bliss for parents who don't want their kid binging on sugar
and salt. The fact that they use just three ingredients makes them
even more awesome.

10 pitted dates

120 g (1¼ cups) almond meal

45 g (½ cup) desiccated
coconut, plus extra for rolling

Makes 10

GF DF EF VG

First thing's first, we need to soften the dates. The best way to do this is to put them in a heatproof bowl and cover them with boiling water. Let them sit for about 20 minutes. Drain the dates and drop them into a food processor with the remaining ingredients. Blitz until all the ingredients are combined.

Place enough desiccated coconut for rolling on a plate.

Use a tablespoon to scoop out some of the mixture and with wet hands roll it into a ball. Once you're happy with the shape, drop the ball onto the plate and roll it so it looks like it's covered in snow. Repeat to make 10 bliss balls.

To help them set, pop them in an airtight container and straight into the fridge for a few hours. (However, you can eat them straight away so there's no need to wait that long.)

TIPS

These balls keep in an airtight container in the fridge for 5–7 days. Or freeze for up to 1 month.

Remember to make sure your school allows nuts before packing these in the lunchbox.

SWEET FRUIT STICKS

Fresh fruit on a stick is the best — but add extra vitamins in the form of homemade gummies and it's next-level genius. I made these for my daughter Anela when she was little and she wouldn't touch her vitamin supplements. The fruit gummies need to set overnight, so plan ahead when making them.

125 g strawberries

handful of grapes

handful of blueberries

2 kiwi fruit

¼ rockmelon and/or honeydew melon

8 small wooden skewers

GUMMIES (OPTIONAL)

1 teaspoon melted coconut oil

250 ml (1 cup) cranberry juice

2 tablespoons gelatine powder

vitamin powder (see Tips)

Makes about 8

GF NF DF EF

If you are making the gummies, you'll need a mould or small baking dish to pour the mixture into to set. Brush the coconut oil over your mould or dish.

Pour the cranberry juice and gelatine into a small saucepan over medium–low heat and bring to a simmer, whisking constantly to dissolve the gelatine (and prevent it going claggy and lumpy). When the gelatine has completely dissolved, remove the pan from the heat and whisk in the vitamin powder so it combines evenly. Very quickly, pour the mixture into the mould or dish. Pop it in the fridge to set and harden overnight. When ready, cut the gummies into small circles ready to be skewered.

When you're ready to make the fruit skewers, cut the fruit up into chunks or cute shapes that will easily fit on the skewers — a melon baller is a handy tool to use here. Thread the fruit and gummies, if using, onto the skewers however you like. Sometimes I make the skewers look like rockets as the little peeps love it.

Pop the skewers straight into an airtight lunchbox in a cooler bag with an ice block to keep it nice and cool.

TIPS

Vitamin powder is available at most health-food shops. I use Melrose Health Super Green powder. Be guided by the instructions on the bottle as to how much you add to the gummies.

Be sure to snip the points off the wooden skewers with some scissors so that the little peeps don't accidentally stab anyone with them.

Vegan

You can use agar agar in place of the gelatine to make vegan gummies, or simply make the fruit sticks without the gummies.

Fussy eaters

Sub in any fruit your child likes! Watermelon, pineapple and banana are all great options.

PISTACHIO BAKLAVA BALLS

It just wouldn't be right if I didn't include a recipe with a Macedonian twist. Having Macedonian heritage, my mum used to make baklava all the time. My daughter Kiki is a huge fan of these (and I love them with my Macedonian coffee). Make sure you find out the school nut policy before packing these.

150 g (1 cup) unsalted pistachios, shelled, plus 50 g (⅓ cup) extra for dusting

100 g (¾ cup) unsalted walnuts

12 pitted dates

115 g (⅓ cup) honey

1 teaspoon ground cinnamon

Makes 15

GF DF EF V

These are super easy – you just need a good food processor to make this recipe rock.

First, put the 50 g of extra pistachios into the food processor and whiz into a fine powder. Transfer to a plate and set aside.

Drop the remaining ingredients into the food processor and blitz for 60–90 seconds – we want a nice smooth finish, so blitz a little longer if needed to ensure the ingredients have blended well.

Using wet hands, roll the mixture into golf ball–sized balls and then roll them in the powdered pistachio. Pop the balls into an airtight container and refrigerate.

TIPS

The baklava balls will keep in an airtight container in the fridge for 4–5 days. Or freeze for up to 1 month.

Remember to make sure your school allows nuts before packing these in the lunchbox.

Vego/vegan

To make these vegan, swap out the honey for maple syrup.

NO-BAKE VEGAN MUESLI BARS

The whole idea of not having to turn on the oven or air fryer is super awesome to me – the time I save cooking means I can be eating or thinking about eating. This recipe is so easy my kids can make it themselves. If you have younger kids you can help them make it by melting a couple of ingredients for them. Bang! What a win.

270 g (1 cup) tahini

180 g (½ cup) rice malt syrup

250 g (2½ cups) rolled oats

40 g (¼ cup) almonds, crushed

3 tablespoons chopped dried apples

½ teaspoon ground cinnamon

2 tablespoons vegan choc chips (optional)

Makes 10–12

DF EF VG

Line a 20 cm square baking dish with baking paper.

Pour the tahini and rice malt syrup into a microwave-safe bowl. Heat for around 2 minutes, or until the tahini melts into the rice malt syrup.

Place the remaining ingredients except the choc chips in a large mixing bowl and add the tahini and rice malt syrup mixture to the bowl. Stir together really well with a big soup spoon.

Pour the mixture into the baking dish and use the back of the soup spoon to press it down until it's smooth and even. If you're adding the choc chips, sprinkle them on the top, then push them in until they're flush. Pop the tray in the fridge for an hour or so.

Cut the muesli bars into whatever shapes best fit your child's lunchbox.

TIPS

These bars keep in an airtight container in the fridge for 5–7 days. Or freeze for up to 1 month.

Remember to make sure your school allows nuts before packing these in the lunchbox.

Nut free
Use sunflower seeds or pumpkin seeds instead of the almonds.

Gluten free
Use gluten-free oats.

You can take my three-ingredient scones (see page 148) in a sweet or savoury direction – whatever works for you!

I love to make this delicious meat-lovers' frittata (see page 146) the night before, then slice it into wedges for the lunchbox the next day.

BLUEBERRY COCONUT BALLS

Blueberries are my favourite superfood. I use them almost daily in my kids' lunchboxes (a half-handful is enough for a healthy hit). I like to buy blueberries in bulk when they are in season, then freeze them so I can make these beauties year-round.

155 g (1 cup) fresh or frozen blueberries

150 g (1½ cups) rolled oats

1 tablespoon melted coconut oil or MCT oil (see Tips)

1 tablespoon chia seeds

2 tablespoons maple syrup

45 g (½ cup) desiccated coconut

Makes 15

NF DF EF VG

Time to plug in your food processor and blitz some ingredients. Drop in the blueberries, oats, oil, chia seeds, maple syrup and 1 tablespoon of the desiccated coconut. Blitz until all the ingredients are pretty smooth and you want to dip your finger in to taste (but don't do that ... unless no one is watching). Pour the mixture into an airtight container and pop it in the fridge for 2 hours or the freezer for 1 hour.

Place the remaining desiccated coconut onto a small plate or in a bowl. Use a tablespoon to scoop out the cold blueberry mixture, then roll it with your hands until it's almost perfectly round. Roll the ball in the desiccated coconut until it is evenly coated. Repeat until you've used up all the mixture. (If you're like me you'll have to taste test every third one just to make sure the kids will survive.)

These are best popped back into the fridge in an airtight container until you're ready to dispatch them to the lunchbox.

TIPS

Available from supermarkets, MCT (medium-chain triglycerides) oil is great for gut health, the heart and energy levels. It doesn't have a strong taste and is very similar to coconut oil.

These balls can be stored in an airtight container in the fridge for up to 5 days. Or freeze for up to 1 month.

Gluten free
Use gluten-free oats.

CONVERSION CHARTS

Measuring cups and spoons may vary slightly from one country to another, but the difference is generally not enough to affect a recipe. All cup and spoon measures are level.

One Australian metric measuring cup holds 250 ml (8 fl oz), one Australian metric tablespoon holds 20 ml (4 teaspoons) and one Australian metric teaspoon holds 5 ml. North America, New Zealand and the UK use a 15 ml (3-teaspoon) tablespoon.

LENGTH

METRIC	IMPERIAL
3 mm	⅛ inch
6 mm	¼ inch
1 cm	½ inch
2.5 cm	1 inch
5 cm	2 inches
18 cm	7 inches
20 cm	8 inches
23 cm	9 inches
25 cm	10 inches
30 cm	12 inches

LIQUID MEASURES

ONE AMERICAN PINT	ONE IMPERIAL PINT
500 ml (16 fl oz)	600 ml (20 fl oz)

CUP	METRIC	IMPERIAL
⅛ cup	30 ml	1 fl oz
¼ cup	60 ml	2 fl oz
⅓ cup	80 ml	2½ fl oz
½ cup	125 ml	4 fl oz
⅔ cup	160 ml	5 fl oz
¾ cup	180 ml	6 fl oz
1 cup	250 ml	8 fl oz
2 cups	500 ml	16 fl oz
2¼ cups	560 ml	20 fl oz
4 cups	1 litre	32 fl oz

DRY MEASURES

The most accurate way to measure dry ingredients is to weigh them. However, if using a cup, add the ingredient loosely to the cup and level with a knife; don't compact the ingredient unless the recipe requests 'firmly packed'.

METRIC	IMPERIAL
15 g	½ oz
30 g	1 oz
60 g	2 oz
125 g	4 oz (¼ lb)
185 g	6 oz
250 g	8 oz (½ lb)
375 g	12 oz (¾ lb)
500 g	16 oz (1 lb)
1 kg	32 oz (2 lb)

OVEN TEMPERATURES

CELSIUS	FAHRENHEIT	CELSIUS	GAS MARK
100°C	200°F	110°C	¼
120°C	250°F	130°C	½
150°C	300°F	140°C	1
160°C	325°F	150°C	2
180°C	350°F	170°C	3
200°C	400°F	180°C	4
220°C	425°F	190°C	5
		200°C	6
		220°C	7
		230°C	8
		240°C	9
		250°C	10

THANK YOU!

The following people deserve a massive shout out – climbing a mountain is easier when others elevate you.

Mary Small
Publisher extraordinaire, you keep giving me opportunities to share my craft and passion. These books that you publish reach people and inspire them to change their little peeps' lunch lives. I can never thank you enough for how much you mean to this dude from Geelong. Love is a strong word: love you, Mary.

Jane Winning
Senior editor with military precision. You set my deadlines and elegantly critique some of my creations; you inspire me to do better each time you're at the helm of my book journey. I think you're a super awesome human and I'm forever in debt to your priceless advice – thank you so much, Jane. No one has ever asked me to change the music on set with such grace.

Martine Lleonart
Copy editor, regardless of what day of the week it was, you were always ready to edit my recipes, your queries were polite and precise and I found working with you almost organically excellent. You rock, Martine. Thank you heaps.

Mark Roper
Photographer dude, man you are the chillest photographer dude I know. I love your work and to be honest I have never liked any of my portraits ever, but you managed to capture me in a way that I'm super stoked with. The recipes and the lunchbox shots look amazing. Who needs photoshop with you around? I honestly hope I get to work with you again, even if it's for my Only Fans (lol). Do you want a Turkish coffee?

Kirsten Jenkins
Food stylist legend. You are super easy and fun to work with, what you brought to set was not what I expected – you, my friend, are next level. Such attention to detail and your work speaks for itself, thank you so very much. And thank you for all the stories. Oh, I almost forgot, do you like my watch?

Meryl Batlle
My right-hand Superwoman. You were so amazing to work with, the most organised and always ahead of schedule. I'm so appreciative of your experience, knowledge and opinion. Oh, by the way, where are the cookie cutters?

Kirby Armstrong
Design guru. This is the fourth book you've done for me and I couldn't be happier. You have really captured the essence of what I do in this design, everything from the layout to the crazy fun colours. Thanks so much.

The Converted Church
What a venue! What a phenomenal setting to shoot my fourth book, the vibe of this amazing 1859 church was mind blowing. I was inspired just being there and my recipes reflect it, too. Thank you.

Kiki

My sidekick, you remind me so much of me when I was your age, you're curious in the kitchen, wanting to create. You always put everyone else first and you spend your last dollar on friends and family. I love you more than you'll ever know and you bring so much joy to me and Mummy. I couldn't do this without you. Daddy loves you forever.

Anela

My first born. From day one you changed my life and inspired me as a dad to be the best I could. I love our chats and our drives when we analyse music and discuss the world. You remind me so much of my sister, your Aunty Suzy, it's like reliving my childhood all over again and I get to be a kid. Daddy loves you more than you'll ever know.

Marine

What can I say? You're the rock of our little family and are super supportive of me living my dream. You're my delicate critic, food taster, advice giver, lover and, most importantly, you're you. Love you x infinity.

Mum

My bestie, you're the best mum. You're my best friend, advice giver and an amazing inspiration. You are the strongest person in the world, you have devoted your whole life to Suzy and me and I see just how much your grandchildren mean to you. You have taught me what love is and how unconditional it is. I can never express how much I love you, how much we all love you.

Dad

The older I get the more and more I look like you. Every morning when I look in the mirror I see your reflection, sometimes I smile and sometimes I cry as missing you doesn't get easier, even after 25 years. You were the smartest, wisest and funniest man I ever knew and I wish I could be a fraction of who you were. I will always love and miss you.

Suzy

My big sister. There's not a day that goes by that we don't talk. We share our emotions and support one another in ways that only we could. Dad taught us that life is too short, and with this lesson we share our ups and downs and always support one another through good times and bad. I'm so happy to see what a wonderful mum and wife you are. Most importantly, you're the best sister ever.

Vince, Lachlan and Julian

Bros, you guys are all super special to me, you have the utmost respect for me and you all treat my family and friends like royalty. Vince, you are the brother I never had. Lachlan, I love how you are discovering the world and the interpretation you deliver, you are an exceptional human. Juju, my not so little mini me, you have grown to become one of the most well-rounded people I know. I can't wait to see you make your mark on this world. Love you all.

Warren Freeman

I could not have picked a better person to share my journey with as a brother. We seem to get it bro, we understand one another in a way that is almost telepathic, we never have a dull moment and our families have intertwined perfectly. What I love about our brotherhood is that we have many years ahead of us with new journeys and memories to create. Love you, brother.

Mini Hippo Team

Megan and Rick, you guys have been the best fresh air to hit me in a long time. Your family business is inspiring and watching the kids get involved the way they do makes me want to work twice as hard for you guys. I feel privileged to be part of the Mini Hippo team and am stoked knowing you deliver products that have truly changed the way we do lunches for the better.

Manse Group

My family away from home, Jake, aka Homie/JP, and Rachel, aka RRP/Signorita. You guys have been super amazing to me, giving me the time off to pursue my passion but, most importantly, giving me the opportunity to grow and develop. You are truly a next-level couple running a top-notch company with an awesome crew. JP, I guess we are just AS1684.2 Section 6.3.2.1.

Meeko

I wish you could read this little man. I love cooking every single meal for you and you never ever complain, you just wag that tail of yours and eat. You have changed the dynamic of our house and bring us all so much joy and love. We couldn't imagine life without you, Meeks.

Lil Peep

Your music changed my tune in life, in my opinion you're the most talented musician since Eddie Vedder and Kurt Cobain. Your music has soothed my soul at a time when I needed it, and at other times when I just want to rock out in my car. Thank you, Gus.

INDEX

Pan Macmillan acknowledges the Traditional Custodians of country throughout Australia and their connections to lands, waters and communities. We pay our respect to Elders past and present and extend that respect to all Aboriginal and Torres Strait Islander peoples today. We honour more than sixty thousand years of storytelling, art and culture.

A Plum book

First published in 2023 by
Pan Macmillan Australia Pty Limited
Level 25, 1 Market Street,
Sydney, NSW 2000, Australia

Level 3, 112 Wellington Parade,
East Melbourne, VIC 3002, Australia

Text copyright © George Georgievski 2023
Design Kirby Armstrong copyright © Pan Macmillan 2023
Photographs Mark Roper copyright © Pan Macmillan 2023

The moral right of the author has been asserted.

Design and typesetting by Kirby Armstrong
Editing by Martine Lleonart
Index by Helena Holmgren
Photography by Mark Roper
Prop and food styling by Kirsten Jenkins
Food preparation by George Georgievski and Meryl Batlle
Colour reproduction by Splitting Image Colour Studio
Printed and bound in China by 1010 Printing International Limited

A CIP catalogue record for this book is available from the National Library of Australia.

We advise that the information contained in this book does not negate personal responsibility on the part of the reader for their own health and safety. It is recommended that individually tailored advice is sought from your healthcare or medical professional. The publishers and their respective employees, agents and authors are not liable for injuries or damage occasioned to any person as a result of reading or following the information contained in this book.

The publisher would like to thank Mini Hippo for their generosity in providing props for the book.

10 9 8 7 6 5 4 3 2 1

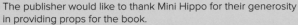

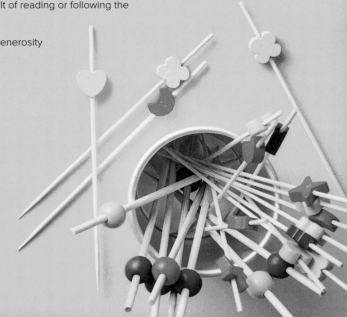